Vol 1

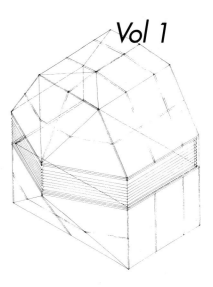

2

Building 8: Edmond & Corrigan at RMIT.

Bibliography.
Includes index.
ISBN 1 86395 314 0 (v. 1.).
ISBN 1 86395 315 9 (v.2.).
ISBN 1 86395 316 7 (v. 3.).
ISBN 1 86395 313 2 (set).

1. Edmond & Corrigan. 2. Royal Melbourne Institute of Technology - Buildings. 3. Universities and colleges - Victoria - Melbourne - Buildings. I. Corrigan, Peter, II. Edmond, Maggie. III. Title: Building Eight.

727.3099451

Building 8: Edmond & Corrigan at RMIT.

Executive Editor, Leon van Schaik
vol 1 - 10 Essays
Edited by Leon van Schaik & Nigel Bertram
vol 2 - Design Development
Edited by Nigel Bertram
vol 3 - The Writings of Peter Corrigan & Maggie Edmond
Edited by Winsome Callister

© 1996 Schwartz Transition Monographs, Melbourne
Published in Australia in 1996 by
Schwartz Transition Monographs
Level 4/325 Flinders Lane, Melbourne, 3000, Victoria, Australia

Made in Australia

BUILDING 8

Edmond & Corrigan at RMIT

vol 1

10 Essays

vol 2

Design Development

vol 3

The Writings of Peter Corrigan & Maggie Edmond

Vol 1

TEN ESSAYS
Edited by Leon van Schaik
and Nigel Bertram

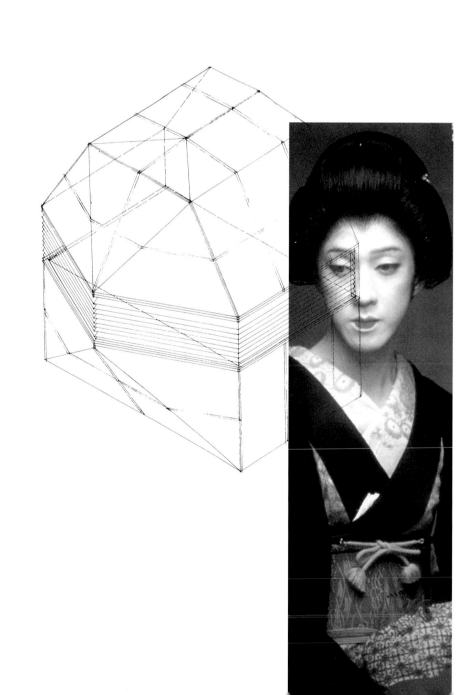

executive editor
Leon van Schaik

editor volumes 1 & 2
Nigel Bertram

editor volume 3
Winsome Callister

style editor
Brenda Marshall

design & layout
Callum Fraser

model photography
Christian Shiel

thanks to
Bronwen Jacobs, Mark Van Den Enden, Peter Saide

sponsors
Franco Belgiorno-Nettis

Karl Fender

Bob Nation

Peter Slattery

Leon van Schaik

Foreword

Often encountered is the problem of what it is that lifts the work done by a professional out of the ordinary run of competence that professionalism entails. Having a view of what the good society might be and pursuing the expression in the work of that view is one modifier: the political sense. Another necessary modifier is connoisseurship: an exhaustive and comparative immersion in a field of human endeavour.

They seem to be a necessary pair. Virtuoso work made without the political sense cloys, evokes the sentimental reaction, resonates only with our surface knowledge. Politically grounded work done without being embedded in a field of connoisseurship is dead-handed propaganda, evokes the sentimental reaction, resonates only with our surface awareness.

To deal with the connoisseur. This is not to be confused with the collector. Susan Sontag's portrait of Hamilton the collector[1] describes the curious joys of finding a way into a set of objects, upgrading the set over time, the delights of the hunt, ownership fulfilled by the completion of the best possible set, with ennui ensuing.

The connoisseur, in contrast, seeks no ownership, but is engaged in an enduring debate about the nature of the ideal evidenced by the imperfect manifestations of the desired admired in the physical realm. Impossible to own all the objects in the set that Colin Rowe compared with one another in his long speculation about the purest ogee, the most attenuated, the most elegant, the most surely proportioned chair.

Impossible to visit, for example, all the plans and elevations of the set of architectural icons that ARM[2] pore over, argue about, see as dim resonances in other works, dream and project into their own new world.

The field, never owned, is never complete. Newly encountered works well up to challenge the connoisseur's classifications, the informal taxonomies that hold the knowledge in the mind. New comparisons or events cast the object-scape into new perspectives that bring unexpected elements into the front of stage.

Once entered a connoisseurial field is an enduring resource, never fulfilled, always extending, always rewarding the attention that is paid. Some make their own work the subject of their connoisseurship, working in multiples and revisiting themes again and again, as do so many artists working in themes (like John Nixon) or architects (like DCM[3]). This endogenous practice strengthens the work in its bones ... the details improve exponentially, the readings become cleaner and clearer. Reworked again and again, the work shakes down onto a surer and surer foundation. For all that, this approach has its problems. Self quotation can replace speculation as the engine of work and merely increasing the scale of a concept can take an idea beyond its capacity.[4]

Exogenous connoisseurship — the obsessive examination of phenomenan outside one's own purview — challenges (in the experimental sense of infecting) the endogenous. Corrigan's enduring interest in sport is such an exogenous connoisseurship. Watching four matches in the 1996 "Lightning Premiership"[5] with Corrigan keeping up a running commentary I learn that for Corrigan and other connoisseurs — even those whose knowledge is forged in one day — the different teams in AFL "footy" display a history in their colours. The teams exhibit spatial behaviour on the field that reveals to the knowing eye the calibre of the thinking that has gone into their concept of the game. Corrigan talks of the "adolescent" game of the Richmond Tigers who pack intense youthful projectile belief into a game in which they clot around the ball wherever it may be in the ingenuous certainty that energy and physically exuberant prowess will force the issue. In contrast, there is the carefully spatial extension of the Fremantle Dockers' game, workmanlike covering of the terrain with "quality circles" so that where the ball might be there always one of them also will be. Here is the mature suspension of gratification approach foreign to the adolescent mind. Thus the characteristics of each team are teased out by numerous acts of careful observation, rumination and discussion until there exists for Corrigan a taxonomy of probabilities that he as connoisseur can dream through. Then on this base of probabilities there arises speculation about those individuals whose character captures the imagination — tales of origins and past triumphs and characteristics that could lead you to expect a response from them of such and such a kind. Julian Kirzner's arm out sensing the opposition full-back's position, eyes always on the ball, ballet in the goal mouth rewarded by the moment of a "mark"; Kickett's von Guerardian attenuated extremities extending to connect improbably with the flailing unpredictable projectile, hair streaming vector to his movement.

This would be entertaining indulgence were it not set into a political frame.[6] Colin Rowe's obsession

with chairs paralleled his extraordinary ability to read cities (usually of the old world — we have had to wait for Mario Gandelsonas to reveal that such readings are possible in the new world) in their "figure grounds". His readings from these black and white abstractions had a more than connoisseurial intention. Imbued with Karl Popper's arguments against totalising social programs he searched city grain for proof that "the good city" enshrined variety in its physical make up. In his devastating image of Wiesbaden old and new within a helmet frame, he shows how the variety of micro democratic life is replaced with a "monotopia" in post-war redevelopment. This is a position that has been taken up by Michael Sorkin in his book *Local Codes* in which he seeks to restore the humanist pluralist position in a proposal for radically different codes for districts, each district offering an option...

In Corrigan's connoisseurship of sport there is expressed a deeply humanist politics. The ball sets up random situations that the connoisseur's knowledge is tested by. How will that theory of play work now? How will that player act? Each flight of the ball opens up options for the players, and so often "the wrong option" is the result. As in life, those who are embedded in the game can access the overview only in their mind's eye. Others are in the stands, and they know better, but are not on the field. The cockeyed Platonic "ideal" of life as we live it.

Edmond & Corrigan's connoisseurship is the subject of much speculation in this book. The connections that this speculation posit point to a highly developed involvement in literature (King on Hardy et al) and in architectural theory

[1] S. Sontag, *The Volcano Lover*, Jonathan Cape, London, 1992. See for example ch. 5, pp.65-85.
[2] Ashton Raggatt McDougall Pty. Ltd., Architects, Melbourne.
[3] Denton Corker Marshall Pty. Ltd., Architects, Melbourne.
[4] As in Murcutt's Raheen, and in Sir John Soane's late work, to name but two cases in point, but *not* - no one has remarked upon this - in the case of Building 8.
[5] Rare (1940, 1941, 1943, 1951, 1952, 1963 and then 1996) but exceptionally useful hot-house introductions for those who are new to the game.
[6] While I have understood the homo-eroticism of Duncan Grant's interest in sport (D. B. Turnburgh, *Private: The Erotic Art of Duncan Grant 1885 - 1978*, GMP, London, 1989, pp.8-12), it was not until the Lightening Premiership that I understood the real potency of sport: the way in which it serves as a metaphor for the politics of life. a frame that makes sport such a powerful area for connoisseurship.

(Kohane on the French Romantics et al). Perhaps it is difficult to believe that a single building could be a vessel capable of holding all of this intent. And yet we would not expect anything less from a good novel. Why should not a building narrate as wide a cultural awareness as a book? History is replete with attempts that are as distinguished as the Studiolo of Urbino or as crass as Melnikov's block-cleaved-by-an-axe Palace of the Soviets. In Corrigan's time narrative approaches to architecture were widely explored in the 1960s and early 1970s. For example, some of Tschumi's most innovative architecture is seen in his early work in which he used the methods of Eisenstein (which I introduced to his studio) to explore an architecture more intensely imbued with meaning than had been allowed in architecture since the modern movement eschewed such literal concerns in favour of the industrial machine paradigm. Engines were touted as the social ameliorators, a narrative-free moral high ground still haunted by some who harbour unseemly desires for totalised society. Humanist narrative architecture faded out because no one[7] developed a political frame to show how a practice that seemed irredeemably elitist could in fact be populist to exactly the same extent that it appeared to rely on inside knowledge for its "reading". The re-discovery of Terragni's experiments in *architecture parlante* (The Danteum) sealed narrative architecture's fate as romantically fascist.

It is no mean achievement then that Building 8 heralds a return to "catholic"[8] narration in architecture. Juries awarding Building 8 its various prizes have commented on its urban design, not simply in the traditional frame of street edge and setbacks, but in terms of the way in which the building appears to "read" and express the city around it. The building sets up a dialogue with the streets and lanes about it. Towers are aligned with their terminating axes. Cupolas and windows and friezes and capitals refer to other buildings nearby like Kurakawa's Daimaru, or the exuberant Melbourne City Baths, the neo-classical Storey Hall[9] and the State Library of Victoria, the tiled arcades. Plundering fields of cultural provenance, physical and sporting, it is an urban condenser for its locale.

Is this elitist? Encouraged by Leonie Sandercock,[10] architectural theorist James Holston explores a political frame for narrative despite the fact that this eluded the generation that preceded him. He sees that they abandoned the idea of the dialogue in favour of an architecture of homogenised connoisseurship alone. Tschumi reverted to an aestheticised modern-movement approach in competition with the balefully purist Rem Koolhaas. Cities, Holston argues to the contrary, have a political need to speak of their psycho islands, and express their heterogeneity. This is a way of maintaining democratic health. Giving urban voice to the multicultural presence affirms in physical terms the ideology of the good city that Rowe also recognised. Such acts of recognition and elucidation reverberate with the cultural systems of the sub groups of the vibrant city. Such architecture provides "spaces of insurgent citizenship". Holston argues that "architects and planners (should) hunt for situations which engage, in practice, the problematic nature of belonging to society and which embody such problems as narratives about the city".[11]

Doesn't Building 8 mark the passage of such groups through our city? Doesn't it speak of the "drawings that we have lived"?[12]

Edmond & Corrigan is itself a multi-cultural partnership: its architecture is of and about "the very heterogeneity of society".[13] "To understand this multiplicity is to learn to read the social against the grain of its typical formations. The typical are the obvious, assumed, normative and routine, and these are the hardest to detect. Rather it is often by their deformations and their counters that we learn about them." Corrigan has remarked that we will all be surprised how soon Building 8 will seem "ordinary". If this happens it will happen because it has captured our realities rather than the sentimental "stock response" (I.A. Richards) of signals such as hearts, tears and large-eyed children and animals. If it succeeds in holding us to our wonderful actualities then we will be able to say of it in Holston's words: "Reading the social against the grain of its typical formations means showing that this surface is indeed doubly-encoded with such possibility (the normative, and its 'countersites' and 'counterforms')".[14]

In this volume Kohane, Bertram, Selenitsch, Goad, Kohane, Hocking, Bremner and King exercise their own connoisseurial visions of Building 8. These speculations are followed by a revealing interview between Michael Anderson and Peter Corrigan (far too revealing, Corrigan remarks) and as editor I conclude with a discussion of the nature of RMIT as client.

Kohane, who graduated from Melbourne University and was educated at Penn, sets the scene for the work of Edmond & Corrigan.

His scholarship allows us to perceive the intellectual milieu that pervaded Yale during Corrigan's first American sojourn. Corrigan, who together with many of his compatriots describes his time at Melbourne University as an experience that forced him into autodidactic mode, denies conscious awareness of much of this world. But the people that he met and drank with were working in these fields, and the critics he encountered were grappling with the re-discovery of British and French romanticism as the Puritan zealotry of modernism faded.

Bertram, also a graduate of Melbourne University, educated in Edmond & Corrigan's office during the design of Building 8, describes the history of Building 8's urban context, and reveals an intense stream of modernist intentions leading up to the construction in 1976 of John Andrews' heroic Union Building. As in jujitsu, Building 8 gathers much of its power from the leverage it exerts on the noble fragment of John Andrews' vision. I fancy that it also works off against the rationalist visions of the master-plans that found partial realisation in Buildings 10, 12 and 14.

The full extent of the difference between the rationalist planning of the 1970s, and the humanist irony of Edmond & Corrigan is apparent in the plans of the building, which until this analysis by Alex Selenitsch, have been far too little remarked upon. The almost organic village plans bulge and cascade about the program which shifted radically up to within six weeks of the fit-out of any given floor, and which Corrigan knows full well are destined to flow for the rest of the life of the building.

[7] I did have a go in two unpublished theses at the AA in "Descent into the Street", 1969, and West London Project, 1970.

[8] The senses of encoding and of wide inclusion both work here.

[9] We will always have to remind ourselves that the design of Building 8 preceded the design for the restoration of Storey Hall by Ashton Raggatt Mc Dougall.

[10] Leonie Sandercock (ed), "Making the Invisible Visible New Historiographies for Planning", Planning Theory 13, Franco Angeli, Milan, Summer 1995, pp.35-51.

[11] Note Peter King's point about the visible in the "wall" of Building 8.

[12] G. Bachelard, The Poetic's of Space, Beacon Press, Boston, 1969, pp.11-12, 1994 ed.

[13] L.Sandercock, Op. Cit.

[14] Ibid.

Philip Goad then gives us an irreverent snapshot of life in the office during the design period, the veracity of which can be attested to only by the many talented young architects who have conducted their rites of passage in Little La Trobe Street since 1976. This office has served as a social condenser for architectural ambition since its inception.

Kohane returns to relate Building 8 to his scholarly investigation into polychromy in architecture. He argues that Building 8 contributes to current architectural debates because it sustains interest in the power of built form to communicate with an audience of city dwellers. He concludes that "at RMIT, Edmond & Corrigan have designed a building with strong legs, colourful clothing and sparkling, eye-like windows to capture the attention of city-dwellers, offering them a vision of a more vibrant, rhetorical and spiritual life. Respecting the theoretical relationship between decoration and decorum, the building has been conceived in terms of a social transaction, an appropriately ornate gift from RMIT to the community of citizens."

Jennifer Hocking, using her Princeton eyes, analyses the remarkable relationship between Andrews' building, "representative" of the modernist dialogue" and proposes that Building 8 "flows out of the violent oppression caused by the modern condition". She finds it an "extension, not a replacement, of this framework".

Domus Academy Master Craig Bremner considers the facade of Building 8 as a form of communication "written" on the object.

He notes perceptively the architects' intent that "Building 8's structure has the capacity to adapt itself according to the message sequences that we fashion daily for our navigation of the metropolitan landscape".

Peter King, autodidact par excellence, exposes the politico-connoisseurship of Building 8. He describes how the "distorted memory" of the architecture makes Building 8 "an unlimited field of poetic achievement". The expression of narrative "affirms that life is indwelling in architecture ... what abides in design ... is the apparition of ethics ... Th(is) invisible college is an emblem for behaving in an ethical way in a bloody time: that is its motive".

Like Kohane, Hocking and Bremner, King concentrates on the wall of Building 8, its "woven grammata". For him the facade is laden with recollections from the guild of architecture, Violet le Duc, Wilhelm Wundt, Portoghesi, the Willendorf Venus(!) ... It is a "composition of fragments never torn into space in this way before". He finds that there is a lag effect (hysteresis) that concentrates psychic energy (cathecting) in the wall, the "thin slice ... renewal or re-discovery of the past through which a new future is created". Just as "Architecture Parlante speaks to the city", the "palpable apparition" of its symbols "liquidates space". He finds the facade has a "will to the spiritual" without which the "symbol would not ascend into the invisible".

The essays in this volume are a tribute to more than a building. Revealing perhaps some of the complexity of intention of the discourse that Edmond & Corrigan inhabits is also a tribute to the fullness of the life that can be — should be — led in our city.

Papers

14

Peter Kohane

Everyday Life and Architectural Polychromy: Romanticism and the Buildings of Edmond & Corrigan

1

Edmond & Corrigan's buildings are distinguished by their capacity to shelter as well as engage the affections of their inhabitants. The intention to create architectural settings for an ideal, moral life can be recognised in schemes such as the Church of the Resurrection with its adjacent buildings like the school and housing (Keysborough, 1975-81), the Chapel of St Joseph (Box Hill, 1976-78), Belconnen Community Centre (Belconnen Town Centre, ACT, 1985-88) and RMIT Building 8 (Melbourne, 1990-94).[1] A range of design strategies — from the calculated choice of materials and structural systems to superimposed cladding and incidental ornaments and, most importantly, colour and pattern — engenders a strong sense of community. This interweaving of cultural and design issues represents a unique addition to Australian architecture, and deserves further investigation.

Despite the fact that Edmond & Corrigan's work has had a major impact on Australian architecture over the past two decades, little is known of the theoretical traditions on which the firm draws. This essay seeks to explore the sources and influences which may have inspired Edmond & Corrigan's architectural approach. In particular, I will argue for the crucial importance of Peter Corrigan's years as a Master's student at Yale University. I will also suggest that he may have been predisposed to consider certain ideas current at Yale because of his prior exposure to the ideology of British Romanticism, as articulated by certain influential cultural theorists as well as in celebrated nineteenth—century Melbourne buildings.

During the nineteenth century, British Romantic authors had a major role in shaping an ongoing

Catholic town in 1440.

THE SAME TOWN IN 1840.

literary tradition exploring the meaning of culture. This British culturalist tradition, well-established in Australia, developed within the discipline of English literature, conceived during the nineteenth century as a colonial export.[2] Romantic authors such as William Blake, Robert Southey, William Wordsworth, Samuel Taylor Coleridge, Thomas Carlyle, A. W. N. Pugin and John Ruskin came to represent an elevated domain of culture, capable of impressing readers in countries like Australia and India with a sense of British excellence. Culture in this sense was to have a civilising role. While such a conception was upheld in the twentieth century, an interpretative shift away from its elitism was made in the 1950s by the leftist writer Raymond Williams.[3] For him, the tradition was useful because it provided sources for seeing culture as an idea of a whole way of life for individuals in a community. In his view, culture refers to ordinary values held in common.[4] From this perspective, Australians could identify their own regional way of life, that is, their own culture. One can thus see Corrigan's concern for local values as indebted to the British anti-elitist understanding of culture.

Corrigan would also have been aware of the Romantic contributions to the culturalist tradition through the architectural work and influence in Australia of two major polemicists for the Gothic Revival: the architect and theorist A. W. N. Pugin and the renowned author John Ruskin. Corrigan's debt to Pugin is especially significant because it is based on a shared identity: both are Catholic architects, critical of societies dominated by

Protestant beliefs and utilitarian values. Pugin's cultural and religious critique has been underestimated by historians who refer to his comments on the functional plan and honest use of structure to portray him as an early reformer of corrupt design practices and a central figure in the progressive development of modern architecture.[5] This ignores Pugin's total rejection of modern building technologies and, more broadly, industrial civilisation.[6]

Pugin is important for his role in the culturalist tradition, analysing the dehumanising effects of England's competitive, capitalist society and suggesting an alternative, a vision of life where individuals contribute to their community.[7] This polemic was encapsulated in a famous illustration from the 1841 edition of his book Contrasts: a well-ordered town, the ideal setting for a moral way of life, is set against a view of its current state, the prominent factories and warehouses representing the degraded condition of modern commercial society (fig. 2)[8]. Later British theorists sustained the social critique without invoking Pugin's conservative location of culture in medieval Catholic England. For William Morris and, after him, Raymond Williams, a whole way of life was to be created not by retreating from the present to revive religious beliefs but through progressive politics. Corrigan's work belongs within this culturalist tradition and is creatively inspired by both the Puginian notion of a Catholic community and modern processes and technologies.

1 Henri Labrouste, Drawing inscribed, "Agrigentum". Source: R. Middleton, ed.,*The Beaux-Arts*, Thames & Hudson, London, 1982, pl. II. (original at the Académie d'Architecture, Paris, on loan from Mme Y. Labrouste).

2 A.W.N. Pugin, "Contrasted towns: Catholic town in 1440; the same town in 1840", from *Contrasts; or, a Parallel Between the Noble Edifices of the Fourteenth and Fifteenth Centuries, and Similar Buildings of the Present Day*, 2nd rev. ed. London: Dolman, London, 1841, pl. 1, opposite page 104.

3 William Butterfield, St. Paul's Cathedral (Melbourne, 1880-91). Photo: author.

Living in Melbourne, Corrigan could recognise the influence of Pugin in St Patrick's Cathedral (1858-99) and its ancilliary buildings. Designed by a follower of Pugin, William Wardell, the cathedral is the focus of an assembly of interrelated Catholic buildings which once included a school. A precinct comprised of hierarchically organised buildings is established. Although the grid defines the site's perimeter, the edge is here subordinate to the cathedral. The key to this self-contained character is the cathedral's orientation, which does not respect Melbourne's pervasive grid. Such a disjunction calls attention to two opposed urban conceptions. The grid suggests infinite extension and facilitates economic and urban growth. It is open to the future and encapsulates dominant utilitarian values. By contrast, the cathedral and its subordinate buildings involve notions of centre, edge and hierarchy. The openness here is not to the future but to the medieval past and the idea of an organic, social and religious order.[9] From her reading of Raymond Williams' Culture and Society, 1780-1950, the urban theorist Françoise Choay coined terms applicable to this contrast: the grid and cathedral complex refer respectively to "progressist" and "culturalist" models of urban form.[10]

The most important recent realisation of the "culturalist" model in Australia is Edmond & Corrigan's complex of buildings constructed between 1974 and 1981 in the outer Melbourne suburb of Keysborough. Again, the grid defines the boundary but not the siting and massing of the series of related buildings constructed over an extended period of time: the Church of the Resurrection (1975-77); Parish Centre (1974-75); School (Stage 1: 1975-77; Stage 2: 1976-78); Hall and Teenage Centre (1978-81); and Caroline Chisholm Terrace housing for the elderly (1977-79).[11] Each individual building possesses a distinct character, created by massing, colour and attached ornament. These architectural qualities, often drawn from the surrounding suburban context, are intended to ensure effective communication with the beholder, enhancing a sense of belonging to a unique place. Tradition is respected in the design of the buildings as well as the institutions of religion, education and domesticity they shelter. Edmond & Corrigan has created a precinct where beliefs and rituals with diminished relevance elsewhere can flourish in novel ways. Conceived as a setting for a whole way of life for individuals in a society, the Keysborough complex can be related to the interwoven conservative and radical themes which characterise the culturalist tradition. To sum up, then, one can discern the relevance of Pugin's Catholicism and medievalism as well as the twentieth-century leftist notion that culture is ordinary to Corrigan's populism and view that values held in common are the source of an organic community.

Nevertheless, Pugin and the British culturalist tradition have been more important to Corrigan's understanding of community than to his design strategies. Pugin's definition of imitation and ornament, for instance, are too narrow to be of assistance. His call for the imitation of a single style, English fifteenth-century Gothic, conflicts with Corrigan's eclecticism, which refers to many past and present buildings. Furthermore, Edmond & Corrigan's vigorously juxtaposed volumes, structural systems and ornaments contradict Pugin's dictum that "all ornament should consist of enrichment of the essential construction of the building".[12] Completely misread by Robert Venturi, Denise Scott Brown and Stephen Izenour to support their "Decorated Shed", Pugin's stance reinforces a purity and logic of style where ornament is acceptable only as the embellishment of a structural element.[13]

Instead, Corrigan's eclecticism and use of colour is influenced by other nineteenth century British theorists and architects who reconfigured many of Pugin's ideas for a larger, non-Catholic audience. In this latter phase of the Gothic Revival, known as the High Victorian Gothic movement, architects strove to develop a striking urban architecture through both a synthesis of past styles and the use of colour.[14] Ruskin's widely read The Stones of Venice (1851-53) poetically encapsulated the movement's principles.[15] Interested in reading the past as a key to understanding the present, Ruskin

believed Venice was a type of modern London. He described the Ducal Palace as the "central building of the world".[16] Distinct cultural traditions flowed to Venice where they formed eddies and momentarily came to rest. Out of this mixing of traditions, Venetians constructed their Ducal Palace. For Ruskin, an architectural style was not created as an ultimate resolution of hitherto unresolved contradictions in a single tradition.[17] Instead, he praised the Ducal Palace for its very impurity of style, which locates the building within the flux of time and traditions.

The architects Ruskin admired, such as William Butterfield and G. E. Street, were already creating their own interpretations of the Ducal Palace, eclectic and imperialistic "central buildings of the world" for London, Britain and its empire.[18] Butterfield, an Anglican architect, designed the first major example of High Victorian Gothic in 1849, with the vibrant brick church of All Saints, Margaret Street, London. His scheme of 1880 for St Paul's Cathedral (built between 1880-91) in Melbourne synthesised an English Gothic plan, polychromatic striped masonry bands from Siena Cathedral, and classical horizontality (fig. 3). High Victorian Gothic qualities of eclecticism and colour also appeared in commercial architecture, like Melbourne's "boom period" Rialto and Olderfleet buildings, both designed by William Pitt in 1889.[19] These sources — the writings of Ruskin and Melbourne's Anglican and commercial Gothic buildings — could inspire Corrigan's interest in eclectic architecture. Like Ruskin's Venice, Corrigan's Melbourne is home to many traditions which constantly interact and transform themselves. Edmond & Corrigan's architecture has always participated in and has renewed this historical flux and vitality.

From the foregoing analysis, one could suggest that Corrigan was prepared to take advantage of the intellectual ferment prevailing at Yale

I would like to thank Louise Marshall and Nigel Bertram for their helpful comments on the text.

[1] These buildings are illustrated in C. Hamann, Cities of Hope. Australian Architecture and Design by Edmond and Corrigan 1962-92, Oxford University Press, Melbourne, 1993, figs. 42, 48-88, 93-103, 181-90 and 238-49. Hamann has also analysed Edmond & Corrigan's buildings from the perspective of the client and users.

[2] See G. Viswanathan, The Masks of Conquest: Literary Studies and British Rule in India, Columbia University Press, New York, 1989; and E. Said, Culture and Imperialism, Vintage, New York, 1994, pp.48 ff.

[3] The most important book from this decade is R. Williams, Culture and Society, 1780-1950 (1958), Penguin, Harmondsworth, 1971.

[4] See R. Williams, "Culture is Ordinary" (1958) and "The Idea of a Common Culture" (1968), in Resources of Hope: Culture, Democracy, Socialism, ed. R. Gable, Verso, London, 1989, pp.3-18, 32-8.

[5] Although Nikolas Pevsner did not discuss Pugin in detail in his widely read Pioneers of Modern Design from William Morris to Walter Gropius (1936), Penguin, Harmondsworth, 1960, this book created the historical framework for seeing Pugin as one of the precursors of the modern movement.

[6] This makes Pugin less the precursor of Walter Gropius and Mies van der Rohe, and more a source for Leon Krier.

[7] Pugin's theory and its debt to Romantic writers like Carlyle and Coleridge is discussed in P. Stanton, "The Sources of Pugin's Contrasts", in Concerning Architecture. Essays on Architectural Writers and Writing Presented to Nikolaus Pevsner, ed. J. Summerson, Allen Lane, London, 1968, pp.120-39. The best introduction to his architecture is P. Stanton, Pugin, Thames & Hudson, London, 1971.

[8] The illustration is titled "Contrasted towns: Catholic town in 1440; the same town in 1840". See A.W.N. Pugin, Contrasts; or, a Parallel Between the Noble Edifices of the Fourteenth and Fifteenth Centuries, and Similar Buildings of the Present Day, 2nd rev. ed., Dolman, London, 1841, pl.1, opposite p.104.

9 This issue is discussed in K. Frampton, "The status of man and his objects", in Modern Architecture and the Critical Present. Architectural Design Profile, Academy Editions, London, 1982, pp.6-19.

10 See F. Choay, The Modern City: Planning in the 19th Century, trans. M. Hugo and G.R. Collins, George Braziller, New York, 1969. For Williams' book, see above, n.8.

11 These buildings are discussed and illustrated in Hamann, op cit, pp.50-74.

12 See A.W.N. Pugin, The True Principles of Pointed or Christian Achitecture, John Weale, London, 1841, p.1.

13 See R. Venturi, D. Scott Brown and S. Izenour, Learning From Las Vegas, MIT Press, Cambridge Mass., 1972. For their misreading of Pugin, see J. Rykwert, "Ornament is No Crime", in his The Necessity of Artifice, Rizzoli, New York, 1982, p.101.

14 For an introduction to High Victorian Gothic theory, see S. Muthesius, The High Victorian Movement in Architecture, 1850-1870. Routledge & Kegan Paul, London, 1972.

15 See J. Ruskin, The Stones of Venice (1851-53), in his Works of John Ruskin, ed. E.T. Cook and A. Wedderburn, George Allen and Longmans, Green & Co.,London and New York, 1903-04, Vols. IX, X.

16 See Ibid, Vol. IX, p.38. This topic is discussed in D.B. Brownlee, The Law Courts. The Architecture of George Edmund Street, The Architectural History Foundation, New York, 1984, pp.17-35, esp. p.26.

17 A highly regarded account of the Gothic style in terms of such a resolution is E. Panofsky, Gothic Architecture and Scholasticism, Meridian, Cleveland and New York, 1957.

18 Butterfield's architecture is discussed in P. Thompson, William Butterfield. Victorian Architect, M.I.T. Press, Cambridge, Mass., 1971. Street's theory was outlined in G.E. Street, "True Principles of Architecture and the Possibility of Development", Ecclesiologist, August, 1852, pp.247-62. This is analysed in Brownlee, op cit.

19 Another building in the same block of Collins Street is the South Australian Insurance Building (Oakden, Addison & Kemp, 1888). Although the Melbourne examples and numerous other buildings in Australia, Britain and America belong to a style termed "Ruskinian Gothic", it was too commercial and popular for Ruskin, who publicly regretted his influence. On the style, see M.W. Brooks, John Ruskin and Victorian Architecture, Rutgers University Press, New Brunswick, 1987.

20 R. Venturi, Complexity and Contradiction in Architecture, Museum of Modern Art, New York, 1966. Venturi's influence on Corrigan has been documented in Hamann, op cit, pp.31-34.

21 For Scully's defense of Venturi, see his "Introduction" to Venturi's Complexity and Contradiction, op cit, The most important interpretation of an American tradition is V. Scully, American Architecture and Urbanism, Thames & Hudson, London, 1969.

22 See R. Venturi, D. Scott Brown and S. Izenour, Learning from Las Vegas, op cit, and Signs of Life, Aperture, New York, 1976, pp. 49-65. The exhibition was displayed at the Renwick Gallery, National Collection of the Fine Arts, Smithson Institution, Washington DC. in 1976.

23 See J.G. von Herder, Reflections on the Philosophy of the History of Mankind, ed. F. E. Manuel, University of Chicago Press, Chicago, 1968 (first published 1784-91).

24 See V. Scully, op cit, pp.92ff; 99ff; 104ff; 212ff; and 229-41. Scully was building upon earlier histories of architecture influenced by American Romantic authors like Henri Thoreau and Ralph Waldo Emerson. For Scully, the most significant history was written by the critic of culture and technology, Lewis Mumford. See his The Brown Decades: a Study of the Arts in America, 1865-1895, 2nd rev. ed., Dover, New York, 1955.

25 See Scully, op cit, pp.92-99; 212-23 and 229-41.

26 In discussing Corrigan's "affinity" with ideas of "the Venturis" at Yale, Hamann also notes that "he 'watched [them] from a distance' and stayed out of their Learning from Las Vegas studio."

University and, more generally, on the east coast of America in the late 1960s. In particular, the encounter with the ideas and projects of Venturi and Scott Brown can be seen as crucial in shaping his architectural theory. Corrigan would have already known of Venturi through his first book, Complexity and Contradiction in Architecture (1966).[20] Researched in Rome, this famous manifesto promoted a modern eclectic approach to design through reference to European examples, particularly those from the mannerist and baroque periods. Later, teaching at Yale and supported by the architectural historian Vincent Scully, Venturi addressed the problem of fashioning a distinctly American architecture.[21] This led to an enthusiastic embrace of American traditions, including popular idioms, as sources of design inspiration.[22] Such a strategy was conceived as an alternative to European modernism, seen as an alien import, an overly abstract and universal style which had come to dominate post-war architecture in America. Corrigan's assessment of the problems and potentials of Australian architecture is indebted to this Yale critique of modernism and defense of national or regional traditions.

Corrigan may well have been receptive to debates at Yale because they reinforced his understanding of culture and accompanying interest in British Romanticism. With a broader historical perspective that embraced European Romanticism in general, Yale scholars examined early nineteenth century writers and architects who questioned the value of the Enlightenment and French Revolution: universal principles, the Romantics argued, had been promoted at the expense of a sympathetic understanding of the regional and historical forces shaping societies. The consequence was a ruthless eradication of traditions which bind and give meaning to distinct cultures. At the turn of the century, the German romantic historian Johann Gottfried von Herder introduced the relativistic, historicist concept of unique national cultures.[23] Indebted to this philosophy of history, an architect like Pugin could first identify a particular way of life, a culture, existing in pre-Reformation England, and then argue that a return to its stable religious and social hierarchies was necessary to avert a brutal modern revolution on the French model. Other less conservative Romantics stressed that change and innovation were essential to the growth, and therefore the stability, of distinct traditions. At Yale, the nineteenth century Romantic writers and architects formulating ideas in the aftermath of the French Revolution were seen as precursors of designers like Venturi who were responding to modernism. Although separated by 150 years, the Romantics and Venturi questioned the Enlightenment and its legacy by defending unique traditions and cultures.

Corrigan was introduced to an interpretation of American architecture informed by these broad Romantic notions through the lectures and writings of the historian Vincent Scully. Scully admired American architects such as Henry Hobson Richardson, Frank Furness, Louis Sullivan, Frank Lloyd Wright, Louis Kahn and Venturi, arguing that they formed a vital national tradition.[24] Furthermore, he explained how the finest buildings were designed to make a powerful impression on their users. Furness and Kahn achieved this with structural forms, while others, Venturi for instance, relied on ornamental embellishments.[25] These two design approaches were, along with the issues of culture and regionalism, indebted to the Romantic notion that architecture must engage the emotions of those dwelling in a particular community. At Yale, Corrigan could listen to Scully's analysis of American buildings as well as scrutinise novel architectural theories like that of the "Decorated Shed", formulated in Venturi and Scott Brown's Learning from Las Vegas studio.[26] While Corrigan always respected the Puginian, Catholic idea of culture, he had to look beyond Australia and Britain to understand fully the nature of architectural structure, ornament, colour and, ultimately, meaning.

At Yale, then, Scully promoted a continuing American tradition informed by Romantic ideas. As the latest contributors to this tradition, the firm of Venturi, Scott Brown & Rauch explored the role of ornaments attached to structure in conveying specific meanings. In addition, new research into French Romantic theory illuminated the origins of both Scully's American tradition and Venturi's work. While Scully did not focus on French nineteenth century architecture, he guided the work in this field of his student, Neil Levine. Having completed research on Furness in 1967, Levine began a monumental study of the French architect, Henri Labrouste (1801-75).[27]

Levine's analysis showed that Labrouste and his contemporaries, Félix Duban, Louis Duc and A. L. T. Vaudoyer, had radically rejected the universal principles defended by the Académie des Beaux-Arts and its Secrétarie Perpétuel, A.-C. Quatremère de Quincy, turning instead for design inspiration to specifics of place and time, that is, to unique cultures. These French architects, along with Labrouste's most famous pupil, the theorist Eugène Emmanuel Viollet-le-Duc, influenced nineteenth-century Americans like Furness.[28] However, the Romantic theory lost its relevance in France and America by the early twentieth century, a consequence of the powerful Académie and its foremost theoretician, Julien Guadet, who promoted a banal ahistorical doctrine of composition.[29] Little was known of the Romantics' principles until these were re-evaluated by American scholars such as Levine. Several of the principles relevant to Venturi, Scott Brown & Rauch, as well as Corrigan, can be introduced by referring to Labrouste's first significant building, the Bibliothèque Ste. Geneviève (Paris, 1844-50) (figs. 4, 5).

The Bibliothèque Ste. Geneviève had been admired by historians like Siegfied Giedion as a rational, proto-modern building where an innovative exposed iron roof was set within an encasing masonry structure.[30] While not ignoring this, Levine focused on what had previously been considered irrelevant, the ornament and meaning of the building. In his analysis, the structure is now primarily important for supporting paintings, sculpture and, in the case of the external piers and arches, infill panels containing the inscribed names of past and present scholars and writers.[31]

4 Henri Labrouste, Bibliothèque Sainte-Geneviève (Paris, 1844-50). Elevation detail and section of wall, Source: A. Drexler, ed., *The Architecture of the Ecole des Beaux-Arts*, MIT Press, Cambridge, Mass., 1977, p.339. (Original in the Bibliothèque Nationale, Paris).

5 Henri Labrouste, Bibliothèque Sainte-Geneviève (Paris, 1844-50). Interior. Photo: author.

6 Henri Labrouste, Restoration drawing of the "Basilica", Paestum, 1828-9, interior perspective. Source: R. Middleton, ed.,*The Beaux-Arts*, Thames and Hudson, London, 1982, ill.123, p.147. (Original at the Ecole des Beaux-Arts, Paris).

7 Henri Labrouste, detail from "Agrigentum".

Modernity was expressed in both the iron structure and, more importantly, writing, seen by Labrouste as the dominant medium of communication in an age characterised by the vast production of printed texts and mass literacy. The supported ornaments literally spelt out the meaning of the library to a now literate public. With a rational structure serving as the scaffold for highly articulate ornaments, the building expressed its culture in forms popularly understood.

Levine linked Labrouste to the Romantic movement by showing how he helped Victor Hugo with the chapter "This will kill that", written in 1830 for a new edition of The Hunchback of Notre-Dame.[32] In this, Hugo investigated the impact of the printing press on architectural meaning, spelling out the problems a modern architecture faced when the built fabric itself could no longer be conceived or experienced as a symbolic language. Labrouste's later architectural response was a library where the structure was the scaffold, the mere blank page awaiting the addition of ornaments and inscriptions. These were meaningful because they could be read. Levine's historical analysis of the Bibliothèque Ste. Geneviève reinforced current thinking at Yale on culture, architectural structure and ornament, as well as the explicit communication of meaning.

Levine, along with another American historian, David Van Zanten, also examined the initial formulation of French Romantic architectural theory in student projects from the 1820s. In this decade, Labrouste, Duban, Duc and Vaudoyer won the Grand Prix de Rome and therefore left Paris to spend five years as pensionnaires completing their studies. Based at the French Academy in Rome, they were required to send envois, drawings of historical buildings or new designs, to Paris each year. The most profound and radical were reconstructions of ancient buildings. As had been the case since at least the Renaissance, a new interpretation of antiquity carried with it a transformation in architectural theory. With their envois, the pensionnaires countered the traditional academic belief that the ancients had created ideal, universally valid forms, arguing instead that buildings were unique expressions of historical and regional contexts.

Labrouste's fourth year envois of 1828-29 focused on Paestum, the Greek colony south of Rome. Ignoring ideal principles, and sympathetic to the Romantic conception of culture, which he may have known through Herder,[33] Labrouste's series of drawings and accompanying text described particular events in the life of the colonists.[34] He argued that the Greeks, having survived the sea journey, would first build a temple dedicated to Neptune. The ensuing task of farming was

accompanied by building the Temple of Ceres. Finally, a civic building was needed, the assembly hall or "Basilica". This imaginative reconstruction of a community, its history and its three major buildings, was diametrically opposed to the academic defence of the orders as the embodiment of correct proportion. According to the Académie, the delicately proportioned Temple of Neptune was constructed last, the culmination of that gradual process of refinement found in Greece, which ultimately determined the ideal type.

Labrouste's rejection of this whole topic of proportion and interest instead in culture with its everyday activities is encapsulated in a small interior perspective of his "Basilica" (fig. 6).[35] Here, the orders have no representational value and merely form part of the structural scaffold which supports meaningful additions. Inscriptions on the orders and walls, as well as shields and spears pinned to the roof structure, speak clearly and directly to the community of recent battles and other concerns of general interest.

In 1828 Labrouste also made a remarkable illustration of a Greek hill town which although titled "Agrigentum" bears little resemblance to this colony in Sicily (figs. 1, 7).[36] A Romantic fascination with layers or accretions of colourful forms is expressed more vividly here than in the Paestum envois and the Bibliothèque Ste.

Geneviève. Labrouste portrays the city wall and its prominent gate enclosing three major buildings. At the right is a palace with two superimposed pillastraded loggias, the lower one supporting a curtain. To the left are a tomb, coloured red with a blue pyramidal roof and attached representation of the deceased, and a pedimented Doric temple. The city is composed of several non-canonical, polychromatic structures. Labrouste also suggests that the architectural colour and impurity of form have their source in daily life and the search for appropriate symbols. The outer wall and inner terrace have crenellations painted red and blue respectively which, as Van Zanten notes, are probably intended as a defensive charm, similar to the coloured rings of fortifications known through Herodotus' description of Ecbatana.[37] Such a symbolic charm is reinforced by the gate where shields, spears and a chariot wheel from a recent battle are proudly displayed to ward off enemies.

While the battle spoils also appear in the Paestum "Basilica", at "Agrigentum" they are treated in conjunction with the coloured walls to illuminate the significant Romantic architectural principles of accretive polychromy and material transformation. "Agrigentum" is dressed with coloured paint as well as the spoils. The portion of the painted wall between the

See Hamann, op cit, p.31.

[27] See N. A. Levine, "The idea of Frank Furness's Buildings", Masters thesis, Yale University, 1967, and "Architectural Reasoning in the Age of Positivism: the Neo-Grec Idea of Henri Labrouste's Bibliothèque Sainte-Geneviève", Doctoral dissertation, Yale University, 1975.

[28] The importance of French theory to Furness is discussed in J.F. O'Gorman, The Architecture of Frank Furness, Philadelphia Museum of Art, Philadelphia, 1973, pp.14-73.

[29] For debates in the Ecole des Beaux-Arts, see R. Chafee, "The Teaching of Architecture at the Ecole des Beaux-Arts"; D. Van Zanten, "Architectural Compositon at the Ecole des Beaux-Arts from Charles Percier to Charles Garnier"; N. Levine, "The Romantic Idea of Architectural Legibility: Henri Labrouste and the Neo Grec", in The Architecture of the Ecole des Beaux-Arts, ed. A. Drexler, MIT Press, Cambridge, Mass., 1977, pp.60-109, 111-323 and 325-416; D.D. Egbert, The Beaux-Arts Tradition in French Architecture, ed. D. Van Zanten, Princeton University Press, Princeton, 1980; R. Middleton, ed., The Beaux-Arts, Thames & Hudson, London, 1982; and D. Van Zanten, Designing Paris. The Architecture of Duban, Labrouste, Duc, and Vaudoyer, MIT Press, Cambridge, Mass., 1987.

[30] See S. Giedion's chapter, "Henri
Labrouste, Architect-constructor, 1801-
1875", in his Space, Time and Architecture
(1841), 5th ed., Harvard University Press,
Cambridge, Mass., 1967, pp.218-28.

[31] Sculpture, including a representation of
Gutenberg, the inventor of the printing press,
and paintings like the copy of Raphael's
"School of Athens", referred to learning and
scholarship. See N. Levine, "The Book and the
Building: Hugo's theory of Architecture and
Labrouste's Bibliothèque Ste Geneviève", in
The Beaux-Arts, ed. R. Middleton, op cit,
pp.138-73.

[32] See Levine, Ibid, pp.142ff.

[33] Herder's historical method was known in
France from 1816. See Van Zanten, op cit,
p.17.

[34] The Paestum drawings and text are
analysed in Levine, "The Romantic Idea of
Architectural Legibility: Henri Labrouste and
the Neo Grec", op cit, pp.357-93;
Van Zanten, op cit, pp.8-13, 16-7; and
D. Van Zanten, "Architectural Polychromy:
Life in Architecture", in The Beaux-Arts, ed.
R. Middleton, op cit, pp.197-200.

[35] See Levine, Ibid, pp.391-93.

[36] For what follows, see Van Zanten,
Designing Paris, op cit, pp.32-34 and Van
Zanten, "Architectural Polychromy", op cit.

[37] See Van Zanten, op cit, p.199. (The
ancient source is Herodotus, History, Vol.I,
ch. 18).

[38] Van Zanten notes that Labrouste may have
known of such a gate, an Etruscan one with
incised ornament, in Perugia. See his
"Architectural Polychromy", op cit, p.199.
The gate would be the Arch of Augustus
(late second century BC).

[39] See G. Semper, The Four Elements of
Architecture and Other Writings
(1850-51), trans. H. F. Mallgrave and W.
Herrmann, intro. H. F. Mallgrave, Cambridge
University Press, Cambridge, 1989. Semper's
theories are analysed in W. Herrmann,
Gottfried Semper. In Search of Architecture,
MIT Press, Cambridge, Mass., 1984.

spoils and arch of the gate, which includes a frieze of blue triglyphs, is extremely significant. At a later stage in the city's history, this painted frieze, along with the attached spoils, can be removed, but their forms would be retained, imitated as incised or relief ornaments of a reconstructed gate.[38] In this way, the memory of the past and its battle would be enshrined.

Labrouste's "Agrigentum" can therefore be understood on two levels. At first glance it can be read as a slice of life, a description of a moment in time where prosaic materials and objects are used in the walls and other structural elements, as well as their adornments. Thus, the structural forms, built with various kinds of stone, are dressed with painted surfaces, albeit shown peeling off, real battle spoils and the fabrics of the palace. But the polychromatic accretions evoke a further interpretation which transcends this sense of immediacy. Over time the fabrics may be replaced but their forms will be recalled in painted or terracotta surfaces of a permanent wall, while the painted triglyphs and spoils become stone adornments. The ordinary is transformed and the buildings of "Agrigentum" now begin to speak about the past. Perceived as a palimpsest, this city would consolidate the feeling of community by reminding citizens of their shared tradition. A major work of Romanticism, Labrouste's "Agrigentum" shows that the architectural principle of accretive polychromy enhances cultural identity.

Corrigan may also have been aware of the renowned German architect Gottfried Semper, whose mid-nineteenth century archaeological research added to the earlier investigation of Greek buildings by reconsidering the meaning of accretive polychromy. Semper's books, The Four Elements of Architecture (1850-51) and Der Stil (1863, 1867-68), argued that the ancient colourful dressing of the wall, like that in Labrouste's "Agrigentum", was a painted imitation of the archetypal wall, a woven fabric.[39] Semper's speculation on this source

was enhanced by an analogy he drew between clothing the human body and architecture.

Levine's study of Labrouste and the radical interpretation of antiquity revealed the historical source of a distinct approach to architecture, one which several Yale teachers and students were exploring at the time. As has been noted, Scully contributed with his account of American architecture, while Venturi, Scott Brown & Rauch considered American culture and the importance of symbolic ornament. Involved in such debates, Corrigan was directly or indirectly introduced to the architecture of French Romanticism. His prior knowledge of the British Romantics was enriched because Pugin and Ruskin could be located within a broader architectural tradition.

Thus, aspects of the British Gothic Revival could now be related to French Romanticism and Semper. Although Pugin would never admit a debt to the ancient pagan world, the idea of a unique culture entered architectural theory with the 1820s envois of Labrouste and his peers. In Ruskin's Stones of Venice, the architecture of medieval Venice was admired for its colour, formal impurity and eclecticism, the qualities which Labrouste employed in his "Agrigentum" to fashion a setting for everyday life. Ruskin and the High Victorian Gothic movement contributed to the theory of the wall by distinguishing two approaches. One, the Venetian "wall veil"[40] follows the painted surface of "Agrigentum" and Semper's connection of it to woven fabrics. In the other, colour and pattern are created from structural materials. Much admired by High Victorian Gothic architects, this "structural polychromy"[41] appears in the striped interior of Butterfield's St Paul's Cathedral.

Corrigan would have been interested in the influence of Ruskin and French Romantic theories on American architects working in the second half of the nineteenth century. Scully could explain that the most inventive designer,

Furness, integrated these sources in the eclectic and polychromatic Pennsylvania Academy of the Fine Arts in Philadelphia (1871-76).[42] In one of Furness' most impressive spaces, the curved reading room of the Furness Library at the University of Pennsylvania (Philadelphia, 1888-90) (fig. 8), he used an iron roof frame set into a colouful brick and terracotta wall, a structural solution derived from the Bibliothèque Ste. Geneviève and a project Labrouste influenced, Viollet-le-Duc's "Interior of an Assembly Hall", from his Lectures on Architecture, published in the 1870s.[43]

For Edmond & Corrigan, this Romantic tradition — with contributions from French, German, British and American theorists and architects — has had a productive role, informing both the firm's idea of culture and design strategies to express this. With regard to the latter, Romantic sources can be identified for Edmond & Corrigan's treatment of the wall, metal structure and attached ornament, as well as colour and impurity of form.

While the walls of Edmond & Corrigan's buildings are virtually always coloured, different Romantic inspired approaches have been followed. The principle of "structural polychromy" is most often adhered to, with the everyday material of brick used to create patterns.

For the Church of the Resurrection, the dominant colour is red with subdued patterns. Strident contrasts are more common and other Keysborough buildings, such as the Hall and Teenage Centre as well as the two school buildings, exhibit the richness of High Victorian Gothic architecture, specifically the interior of Butterfield's St Paul's Cathedral. In another approach, the varied, colourful surfaces of different buildings in Labrouste's "Agrigentum" are combined by Edmond & Corrigan in single buildings, like the Dandenong College of Technical and Further Education (TAFE) wing (1985-88) and the Athan House, Monbulk (1986-88).[44] At RMIT Building 8, this is achieved with several materials and colours distinguishing front, rear and side facades as well as the roof. The Bowen Street rear itself juxtaposes a High Victorian Gothic stair tower with a pre-cast concrete wall. A third type of wall is related to the painted layers of "Agrigentum", the surfaces that Semper believed represented fabrics. While RMIT Building 8's polychromatic Swanston Street facade may refer to the ancient idea of the wall as a defensive charm or the Biblical account of the wall of the Heavenly Jerusalem, it also can be understood as an imitation in stone of a woven fabric.[45]

In many of Edmond & Corrigan's buildings the space-enclosing masonry wall interacts with a

8 Frank Furness, Furness Library, University of Pennsylvania, Philadelphia (1888-90), interior view of the curved reading room. Source: Progressive Architecture, May 1991, p. 89.

[40] See Ruskin, op cit, Vol. IX, pp.80, 85ff.

[41] See Ibid, Vol. IX, pp.347ff.

[42] This is analysed and illustrated in O'Gorman, op cit, pp.80ff.

[43] The Furness library is illustrated in ibid, pp.164ff. For Viollet-le-Duc's "Assembly Hall", see E.E. Viollet-le-Duc, Lectures on Architecture, (1872; first published London, 1877-81), trans. B. Bucknall, 2 vols, Dover, New York, 1987, Vol. II, lecture 12, fig. 18 and pl.xxii.

[44] These buildings are discussed and illustrated in Hamann, op cit, pp.121-23, 136-39 and figs. 191-98, 230-37.

[45] The Biblical symbolism and the fabric metaphor are considered in P. Kohane, "Clothing the Institution", this volume.

[46] Hamann aptly refers to these as "spectral groin-vaults". See Hamann, op cit, p.81. Like Viollet-le-Duc, Edmond & Corrigan are fascinated by the transformation of slender stone Gothic forms into an equally dynamic and elastic metal structure.

[47] The significance of this dressing of the wall is discussed in P. Kohane, op cit.

[48] The historical references are considered in ibid.

[49] Ideas prevailing in Britain on style, eclecticism, decorum and the picturesque dominated Australian practice in the nineteenth century, the main exception being the German notion of empathy which was valued in the 1880s. On the relationship of these theories to Melbourne architecture, see P. Kohane, "Problems of Meaning in the Late Nineteenth Century: Melbourne's Boom Period Buildings", Masters thesis, University of Melbourne, 1985. By the second decade of the twentieth century, when Australian students were being introduced to French principles, the Ecole des Beaux-Arts had long forgotten its past brush with Romanticism.

dynamic metal structure. This composite structural system is employed to impart an appropriate medieval and religious character to the Chapel of St Joseph. Here, blue painted metal columns, beams and bracing elements support the roofs of the interior and the exterior porch. The juxtaposition with the patterned brick structure is boldly displayed by extending the two central nave beams and columns beyond the external walls. From the outside they appear as Gothic flying buttreses, an image reinforced by the interior diagonal bracing members which refer to the ribs of groin-vaults.[46] Edmond & Corrigan has derived this metal and masonry system from those of the Bibliothèque Ste Geneviève, Viollet-le-Duc's "Assembly Hall" project and the Furness Library. The Furness building was particularly important to the Belconnen Community Centre: the exterior of the Furness Library's stacks informs the external articulation of the Sports Hall, while the curved reading room is echoed in the fenestration and composite structure of the main Youth Centre space. Like Furness, Edmond & Corrigan values the complex structural approach because it adds to the broader Romantic qualities of colour and diversity or impurity of form.

While Edmond & Corrigan's buildings have different structural systems, and the walls can either respect the principle of "structural polychromy" or have a layer of colour, further adornments are always added. Thus, the brick walls of the Church of the Resurrection have attachments like the porch, bay windows and sculpture of Christ on the exterior and religious or everyday artifacts on the interior. At RMIT Building 8, the concrete frame structure is dressed firstly with the tapestry-like stone layer and secondly with incidental ornaments like the oriel windows, silver downpipes and bolts on the two stair towers.[47] Another addition, writing, appears on the Belconnen building. The exterior wall proclaims "Youth Centre" while street signs guide pedestrians within.

The purpose of all such added adornment had been examined by Labrouste. The spoils pinned to buildings in his Paestum envois and "Agrigentum", as well as the writing on the Paestum "Basilica" and Bibliothèque Ste. Geneviève, speak directly to the public in terms commonly understood. For Labrouste, Edmond & Corrigan and Venturi, Scott Brown & Rauch, such symbolic forms create appropriate architectural settings for everyday activities. The firm of Edmond & Corrigan has pursued two approaches. The adornments of the Church of the Resurrection generally derive from the local, suburban context and are legible to the specific Keysborough community. On the other hand, the dressing of RMIT Building 8 has a broad provenance, its cosmopolitan sources engaging the attention of a larger urban public.[48] In both cases, however, the adornments, as well as the walls, roofs and structural systems to which they are attached, have the rhetorical and theatrical role of addressing an audience, that is, a specific community.

Corrigan would have developed his theory at Yale where current architectural thought was clarified, perhaps even shaped, by research into the Romantic critique of the Enlightenment. The focus on French Romanticism was crucial because it not only reinforced Corrigan's social, political and religious convictions indebted to Pugin and British cultural critics but also suggested new design approaches. Seen in this way, the buildings of Edmond & Corrigan have a significant place in the history of Australian architecture: they are a belated introduction of a radical episode in French theory, one which had no direct impact on Australian nineteenth century architecture.[49] Furthermore, it is important to identify the Romantic interpretation of antiquity from the 1820s as the very source of both Edmond & Corrigan's and Venturi, Scott Brown & Rauch's architecture. Indeed, all would accept Labrouste's understanding of the Greek Temple, where the neo-classical vision of perfectly proportioned, white marble forms was replaced by one which delights in formal impurities, especially as created with layers of colourful surfaces, adornments and writing. As the firm of Edmond & Corrigan has shown through its buildings, such architectural qualities create modern settings for everyday, communal activities.

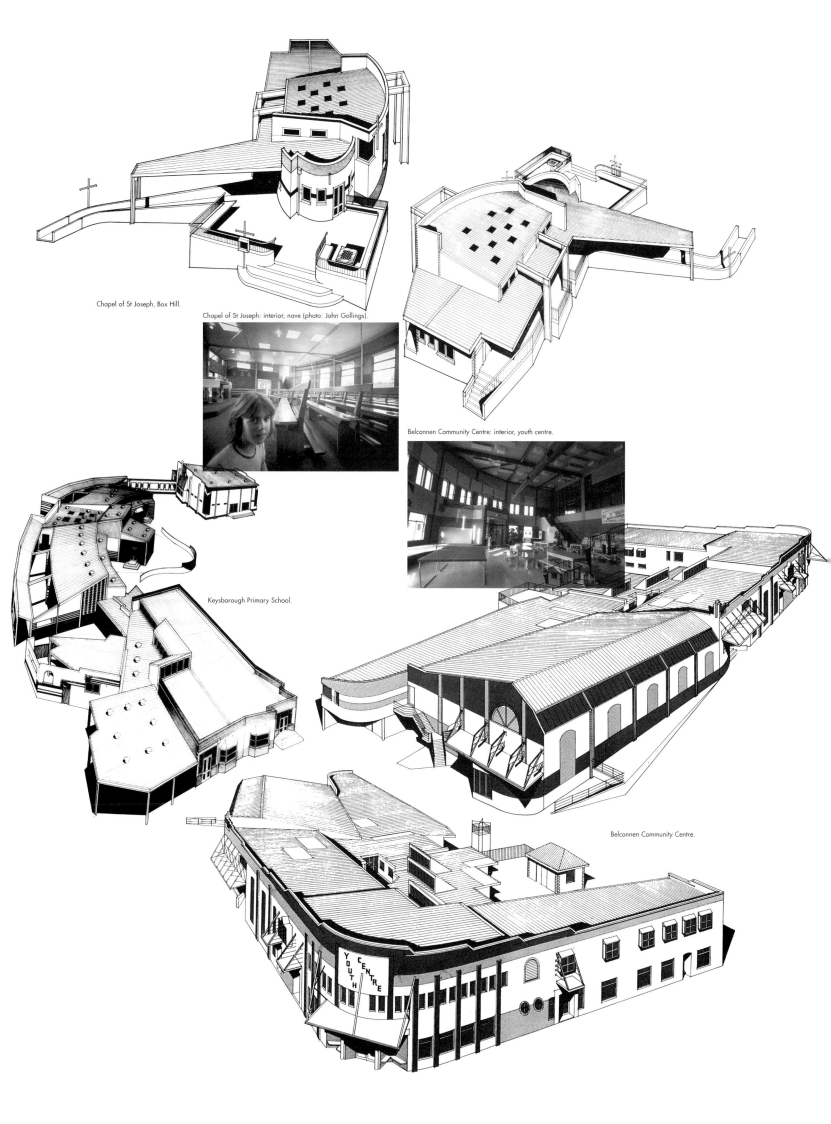

Chapel of St Joseph, Box Hill.

Chapel of St Joseph: interior, nave (photo: John Gollings).

Belconnen Community Centre: interior, youth centre.

Keysborough Primary School.

Belconnen Community Centre.

Nigel Bertram

Institutional Imagings:
Site and Desire in Swanston Street

This paper attempts to locate an architectural understanding of RMIT and its relationship to the city, through an analysis of the physical histories, previous visions and unbuilt strategy plans for the city block on which Building 8 now stands.

The base material is a series of historical images,[1] all of which constitute part of the public and self-image of the institution at a particular point in time. Each image, in its chosen subject(s) and method of representation, communicates certain desires bound up with the projected and perceived self-image of the institution (and also with the image as an object in its own right), whether these desires are fully conscious in the maker of the image or not.

By looking behind the images, so to speak, I hope to tease out some of the complexities, compromises and tensions within this process of image-making and within the dual subjects of institution and city.

1866: The block where RMIT now stands is represented as part of an institutional precinct, a collection of government buildings — the gaol, the Supreme Court, public offices and, on the site of Building 8 itself, the old County Court — located between the State Library and hospital to the south and the City Baths to the north.

The precinct's differentiation from the surrounding commercial city is clear and its mode of operation is that of the government reserve within the speculative grid-city, a paradigm that was overlaid onto the original commercial subdivision of Melbourne.[2]

This representation is in effect the First Master Plan for the site, a plan in which the nineteenth century "City of Knowledge" is inserted into the speculative city of the New World. Its icons are separated from the commercial city by physical setback, topographical elevation and the distance of authority. The concerns of the particular institutions in this case — education, health, law and order — underline the reformist nature of this master plan.

View looking south along Swanston Street, c.1880. The public buildings preach their reformist morals to the sprawling commercial city beyond, their iconic status enhanced by the green verge in front. The concomitant nineteenth century desires of laissez-faire capitalism and social reform are in a relationship of tension across the grid.

2 Swanston Street c.1880, LaTrobe Picture Collection, State Library of Victoria.

5

3

Erosion

This "first master plan", however, was short-lived and already by the mid-1890s, after the demolition of the public offices building, the block's apparent purity is eroded with the introduction of a scattering of commercial buildings on the site. Storey Hall (1887)[3] and the original Working Men's College (1886-91)[4] were built in this period. They coincide with, and perhaps contribute to, a period in which the block is in a state of complexity and confusion, when compared to the singularity of purpose and clarity of the commercial/residential blocks to the west and the institutional blocks to the south.

Fusion

1960: The block has become fused with and indistinguishable from the surrounding city. A series of commercial warehouses built along the Swanston Street frontage from the turn of the century form a uniform facade to the block. As RMIT expands, however, the institutional programme is gradually pushed into the shell of the commercial city so that the boundary between the two becomes blurred, or invisible. By the time this photograph was taken all but a few of the Swanston Street warehouses were occupied by RMIT.[5]

3 1895 map of Melbourne (MMBW) showing current RMIT precinct, Map collection, State Library of Victoria.

4 Aerial view of Melbourne c.1960: the RMIT block is at top right, Harold Paynting Collection, State Library of Victoria.

5 Swanston Street buildings between Franklin and LaTrobe Streets 1965, prior to demolition for the Casey Wing. RMIT archives.

4

Mask

The identities of the block and the institution at this point are hybrid or composite; they are both civic *and* commercial. The form/image has become separated from the content. The erosion of the campus of public buildings of the "first master plan" would appear complete, except that the institutions are still present. In fact for the first time since 1866 the block is again wholly institutional. This momentary state of pure hybridisation (lasting from the time the last warehouse was purchased by RMIT in 1965 to the demolition for the construction of the Casey Wing in 1967) gives rise to the idea of the facade as a mask, and delimits the thin facade of Swanston Street as a site of architectural tension.

Campus

The University of Melbourne, meanwhile, as was common practice in post-enlightenment planning, is located on a large area of land reserved for that purpose from Melbourne's earliest times. It is the quintessential campus, removed from the city as a space of contemplation. The campus model provided both the solid ground and the physical-aesthetic distance required by nineteenth-century thought for the reflection upon and criticism of reality. This is the spatial archetype of the academic's study: the objective datum required for the analysis of data under the scientific, or comparative methods.[6]

In contrast, research at the Working Men's College is carried out on location and its ground-datum is not solid but shifting with the vicissitudes of the city. Subsequent visions of an image or form for the technical institution in the 1960s and 1970s can be seen as attempting to (re)gain the space of the campus within the block; this physical, aesthetic and critical distance that is, conventionally speaking, a position from which one can reflect upon and change the real. These attempts could be read as a desire to give authenticity to an unplanned (illegitimate?) institution that was rapidly evolving into a full-blown polytechnic.

6 University of Melbourne precinct from 1855 map of Melbourne (Kearney), Map collection, State Library of Victoria.

7 Early proposal for RMIT campus redevelopment, RMIT College Council, 1963. Source: Murray-Smith & Dare. Op.Cit..

1963: This desire for the space of the university is communicated in an early vision for the new Swanston Street frontage. In this image, the *whole city* has become a campus, with the large floating block of RMIT running the length of Swanston Street located in a field of dispersal where the city fabric (even the State Library) has all but disappeared.

1967: The point at which the fragile second moment of purity — pure hybridisation — ended, with the construction of the Casey Wing (architects Bates Smart & McCutcheon). The new institutional "face" breaks through the mask-disguise of the city street.

Fortress

The Casey Wing was part of a larger vision, an image of the new institution as a fortress, an unambiguous representation of permanence and strength — all the things that the institution had never had.[7] Within the limits of the appropriated city block, Bates Smart & McCutcheon (BSM) created an image of a campus as serious and aloof physically as the university was culturally and historically. (Claims that the blocks "faced inwards" to provide courtyards onto Bowen Street[8] do not account for the symbolic importance of the Swanston Street frontage, as depicted in publicity images of the scheme.)

The floor levels of these new buildings, three of which were built in the period from 1967 to 1975, do not relate to the level of the Swanston Street footpath. "Ground" level is set in abstract space, which causes a physical disjuncture for the pedestrian in the transition from city space to campus space. This separation of the institution from the lived (walked) city, albeit in a vertical dimension, can be read as an attempt to create the space of the university campus — the critical distance I have spoken of — within the reality of the commercial site. The facade of the BSM scheme is analogous to the ground plane of the university campus. They are both devices of physical detachment.

8 Construction of Casey Wing, 1967, RMIT archives.

9 Proposal for RMIT campus, Bates Smart & McCutcheon, 1965.

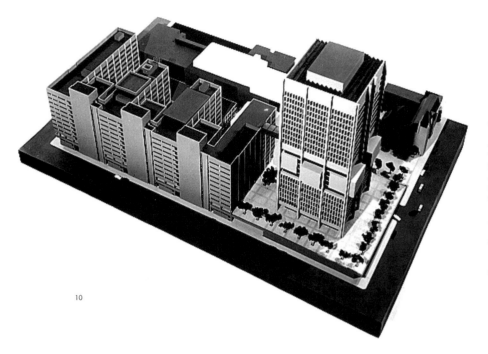

10

[1] I would like to thank the State Library of Victoria, Bates Smart Pty Ltd, John Andrews International, Leith Bartlett Cuthbert Pty Ltd, and RMIT for their permission to reproduce these images.

[2] The original subdivision plans of Melbourne show a uniform division of commercial allotments. This was subsequently overlaid with areas reserved for public or governmental purposes, usually grouping together a number of the standard allotments. It is significant here that the public reserves came after, and had to fit within the logic of the generic subdivision.

[3] Originally Hibernian Hall. Purchased by RMIT in 1954.

[4] Architects Leonard Terry, Percy Oakden and Nahum Barnett.

[5] Stephen Murray-Smith and Anthony J. Dare, The Tech: A Centenary History of the Royal Melbourne Institute of Technology, Hyland House Publishing, 1987, pp.390-92.

[6] An analysis of the difference between .Sir James Frazer's study and Bronislaw Malinowski's tent in the area of anthropological research is made by Stephen Cairns in his paper "Architecture and Anthropology: Three Scenes in a Negotiation", presented at Theatres of Decolonization conference, Chandigarh, India, January 1995.

[7] The physical redevelopment of the city campus in the 1960s and 1970s was closely linked to the Institute's struggle for recognition as an institution providing university-quality education and to the creation of a clearly-defined role and identity within the educational system. In 1960 the Royal Melbourne Technical College, as it was then called, changed its name to the Royal Melbourne Institute of Technology, paving the way for an identity independent of the somewhat restrictive controlling body, the Victoria Institute of Colleges. In 1965, after a protracted battle with the Victorian government and educational bodies, RMIT obtained the right to issue degrees. The recent granting of university status to RMIT, and indeed the construction of Building 8, refurbishment of Storey Hall (Architects Ashton, Raggatt, McDougall) and the future development of the Carlton & United Breweries site at the top of Swanston Street can be seen as a culmination of this long and drawn-out process, providing the campus with a highly significant and tangible presence in the "Knowledge Precinct" of the city. See Murray Smith & Dare, op cit, pp.336-40 and 390-96.

[8] Ibid., p.393.

[9] This point is raised by Carey Lyon in "Unbuilt Melbourne", Transition, No. 24, Autumn 1988, pp.45-49.

[10] An underground tunnel linking Museum Station with the RMIT campus was proposed at one stage.

[11] "RMIT Student Union", Constructional Review, May 1983, p.35. See also Jennifer Hocking, "Building as Event: an Eruption from the Crypt of Modernity", this volume (ed.).

[12] The ideas of both fortress and mask persist in the Edmond & Corrigan facade. The bay windows make it almost harder to see out from the interior than would conventional windows, with confusing reflections of the interior overlaid onto the view from the angled glass, and a gridded seraphic pattern applied to areas of vertical glass. This makes the viewer very aware of the distance between inside and out.

The original Bates Smart & McCutcheon master plan was revised in 1967 to include a twenty-six-storey tower on the corner of Swanston and LaTrobe Streets, opposite the State Library. The tower, a commercial type, was part of the contemporary institutional language, as is shown in Leith & Bartlett's winning entry in the 1965 Civic Design Competition for a new Town Hall precinct on what is now the Melbourne Central site, west of the State Library (fig. 11). In this scheme the Town Hall, in the form of a slab block, shares the same language and is in a balanced composition with the accompanying office tower and shopping emporium/apartments.

Bates Smart & McCutcheon's new RMIT tower would in fact have entered into the composition of these three objects — if both schemes were built — along with interspersed object-fragments of the nineteenth-century city. The previous BSM perspective (fig. 9) shows the corner of a (non-existant) plaza in the left foreground, and seems itself to be a view from a plaza opposite the library. The new RMIT buildings can be seen entering into the picture of the new civic reserve, as part of the same spatial system.

The desire for separation and singularity of the totalising visions represented by BSM's master plans is countered both by the reality of the hybrid condition of the block (in its perpetually "half-completed" state) and by the implied assumption of the inevitability of flux and change in the urban environment contained within the whole ethos of urban renewal.[9] These schemes, which propose the redevelopment of the entire site, somewhat paradoxically also communicate a face of unambiguous permanence and authority. This conflict between the reality of change and the desire for permanence is another manifestation of the tension between the commercial (fluid) and civic (stable) aspirations of the block.

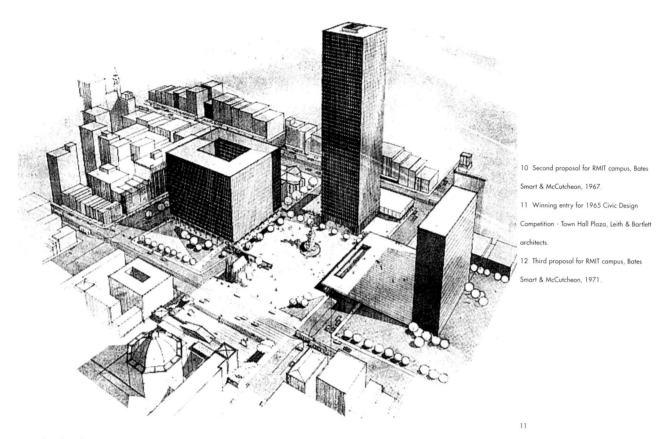

10 Second proposal for RMIT campus, Bates Smart & McCutcheon, 1967.

11 Winning entry for 1965 Civic Design Competition - Town Hall Plaza, Leith & Bartlett architects.

12 Third proposal for RMIT campus, Bates Smart & McCutcheon, 1971.

11

1971: The third version of the Bates Smart & McCutcheon master plan is evidence of a marked shift from the preceding two. The model shows a series of horizontal, transparent plates connected by vertical circulation towers, with arrows indicating vectors of pedestrian circulation and traffic flows through the campus, including a corner entry opposite the future Museum Underground Station, planning for which began in the same year.[10]

The three wings completed from the first BSM plan are represented in stark contrast to the transparency and indeterminate form of the network of "plug-in" infrastructure now proposed, revealing the crisis of form experienced in the late 1960s. This scheme, more transport-interchange than institution, emphasises pedestrian circulation and connections with a distinct horizontality, and in its very representation indicates a desire for transparency and permeability.

This may appear as an absolute departure from the fortress of the first BSM plan and the ideas of separation and distance I have discussed; however, the first (and only) building realised within the mind-set of this "network-city" reveals something more like a sideways shift.

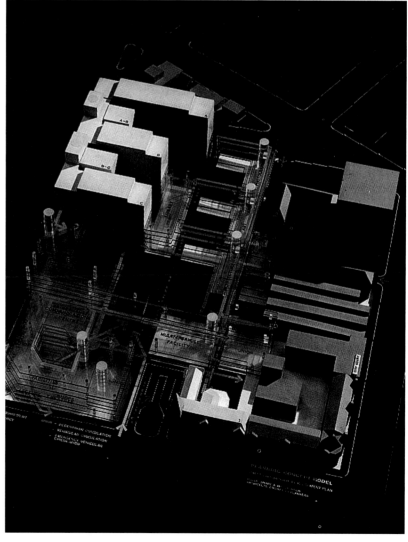

13

14

The RMIT Student Union building was designed in 1977 by architects John Andrews International as a seven-level structure, with the potential for a further five levels of expansion (equal to the built height of Edmond & Corrigan's building). Stage 1 — the first three levels — was completed in 1983 and forms the base on which Edmond & Corrigan's extension now sits. The horizontal plates of the 1971 master plan are expressed on the Swanston Street facade, with the vertical space between infilled with translucent glass blocks, retaining the *image* of transparency but effecting something quite different.

White-Out

An excerpt from a contemporary publication about the building states of the union building that: "The shimmer and movement of people inside is visible to the passerby day and night".[11] In reality the disjuncture is more total. The glass block facades have become a literal screen onto which the shadows of the occupants/the city are projected; the real is abstracted and once-removed into an aesthetic, contemplative experience. Physical connection is achieved (even with the handicap of the inherited abstract floor levels) by traversing the various levels of the campus with ramps and diagonal paths through the site, but visual connections become aestheticised and detached. The desire for the space of the university — the space of contemplation — appears within the white-out of the Swanston Street facade.

This distancing from the city is enhanced by the planimetric erosion of the street line to a forty-five-degree zig-zag pattern. The disruption to the facade-wall of the block gives the impression of a series of pavilions that could be read as discrete objects inhabiting a compressed campus space. The corresponding internal spatial organisation requires a complete re-orientation by the pedestrian upon entering the building from the external logic of the city, adding to the effect of separation, rather than connection.

Accretion

The block as Edmond & Corrigan encounter it in 1990 is quite literally a series of fragments of aborted master plans. What remains after the good intentions of the reformists is a built representation (by default) of the problematic of the institution within the commercial city. The point is that no solution to this dilemma was found; rather, there exists an overloading of thwarted visions, and it is only by accretion that image or identity are achieved at all. This "failure" of all external (imported) models applied to the site, this lack of fit between the vision and the reality, is undoubtedly a condition of utopias in general, as well as an expression of the fickle nature of government education funding, but it also demonstrates an inability to occupy the site.

On one 1855 map of Melbourne, the RMIT block in question is represented, perhaps out of genuine uncertainty, as white space — a void — with the lone County Court building "floating" in empty space. The real and imaginary histories of the site I have outlined might be seen as trying to come to terms with this condition of emptiness. The overlapping plans and visions accrue to give the block a density that would normally be considered uncharacteristic of Melbourne and colonial cities in general, but is, I would argue, emblematic of their particular condition. This is not so much a physical or historical density as a density of dreams.

The facade of Edmond & Corrigan's Building 8 reveals a complex relationship to the conflicting aspirations of the site. It is both a reflection of the city (mirror) and a projection of the interior (screen). It oscillates between opacity and transparency, between Melbourne Central and public building. The ambiguity of this "face" is evident, for example, in the bay windows which read simultaneously as literal projections of the interior space through the facade wall

(a type of "functional expressionism") and as decorative jewels applied to the shiny surface.[12] The facade gives contradictory messages as to whether it is skin or three-dimensional form. This purposeful lack of tectonic consistency and the oscillating identity of the facade reveal an acceptance of the multiple natures of the block and a confidence in the particular characteristics of this institution not present in the previous, more reformist schemes discussed.

The building confirms its position as a fragment at least partially dependent upon its surroundings, with physical gestures to Storey Hall (curved corner) and to the Casey Wing (deflecting facade) as well as multifarious semiotic references. The very fact that the building is perched on top of the old Student Union building — Edmond & Corrigan fought to retain the glass block facades — reinforces this reading. And in a crowning gesture to the compromises and complex nature of the project, grand colonial palm trees — *the* emblem of the civic — occupy meagre planting boxes, restating the institutional garden-setback within the space of John Andrews' 45-degree notches (which was, after all, their purpose).

Edmond & Corrigan's building takes advantage of the dense, overlapping space between the multiple ghosts that have populated the site over the past one hundred and forty years. Its mode of operation is one of opportunism, working between what remains of the heroism and other more contingent pasts to make sense of the remaining pieces as fragments. In doing so, the struggle and aspirations of previous visions remain as "after-images" to the new picture, and the complex identities of institution and block are brought into heightened relief.

13 RMIT Student Union Building (model), John Andrews International, 1977.

14 RMIT Student Union Building, interior, John Andrews International, c.1983.

15 Indicative Building Envelope of John Andrews Scheme (drawing: Edmond & Corrigan).

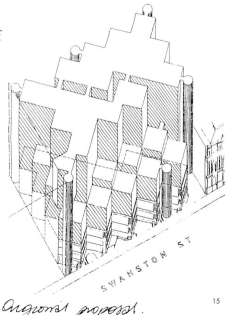

Andrews' proposal.

15

16 RMIT in 1990 prior to construction of Building 8 (photograph courtesy of Ashton Raggatt McDougall).

Inset are proposals for (clockwise from bottom right) Storey Hall Annexe (architects Ashton Raggatt McDougall, completed 1996), Buildings 10,12 & 14 redevelopment (architects McIntyre Appleton Minifie) and Building 8.

Alex Selenitsch

Grid to Polis

Level 1

This composition (or fiction) begins with an examination of the architecture at the site, in its imaginary pre-existing state. Firstly, there is the John Andrews grid which is rotated at forty-five degrees to the street, forming an accordion edge to Swanston Street and trapping a diagonal sweep across the site to Bowen Lane. Secondly, there are the solid orthogonally-placed masonry walls of Building 28 and Storey Hall. Thirdly, there is the gap between Buildings 10 and the Percy Everett building on Bowen Lane on one side, to the north, there are the floor-to-floor heights of the adjacent BSM buildings, a dimension hidden to the planar analysis offered here.

There can be no formal and lucid introduction to this analysis of Building 8. Instead of a text, I have some drawings, or rather, drawings done over the top of other drawings. I wonder whether they might be called meta-drawings, or para-graphics. Perhaps they are marginalia that have wandered into the middle of the page.

In part, they were prompted by some remarks made by Peter Corrigan a few years ago about the graphic qualities of plans and his interest in the kind of marks that architects make on paper. The drawings are also a response to Norman Day's assertion that Building 8 is nothing but a thin facade. For a building that is so many metres thick, with labyrinthian interiors, such an assessment could only be a provocation, a challenge. Whatever the reasons, I took to the plans, floor plate by floor plate, in search of an architectural narrative, something to believe in, however temporary, and this is what I found.

Level 3

At level 3, the first two of these architectural figures are re-framed and enlivened through a contrasting motif. The Andrews grid, originally envisaged as a figure of infinite extension, is stabilised on Swanston Street through a symmetrical location of two new stairs and peripheral columns. The masonry walls of Storey Hall and Building 28 are brought into relief by a wide spiral of columns in variegated section, colour and finish and by a slight rotation of the new external corner against the existing internal corner (although the effect has been compromised a bit by ARM's recent clip-on connections to Storey Hall).

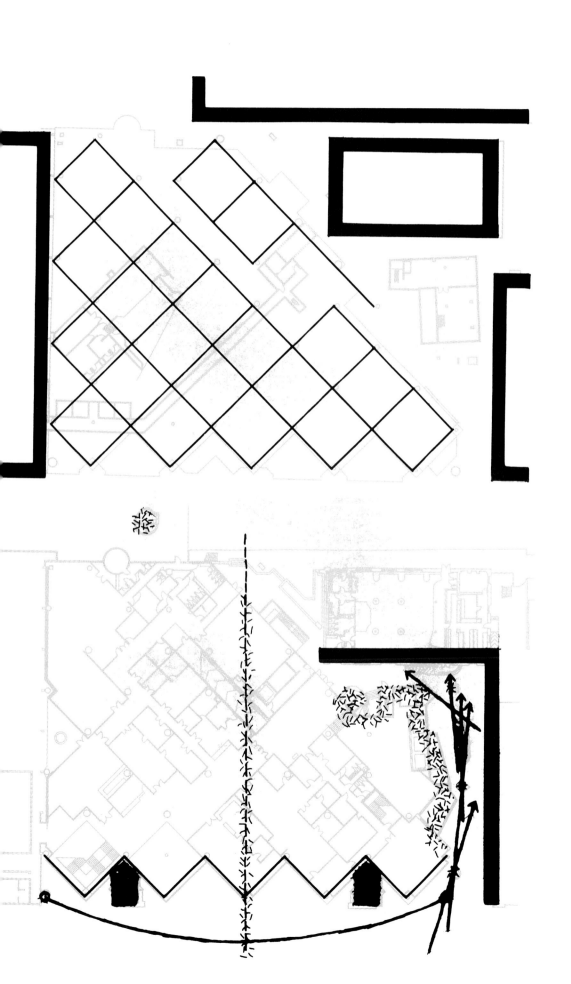

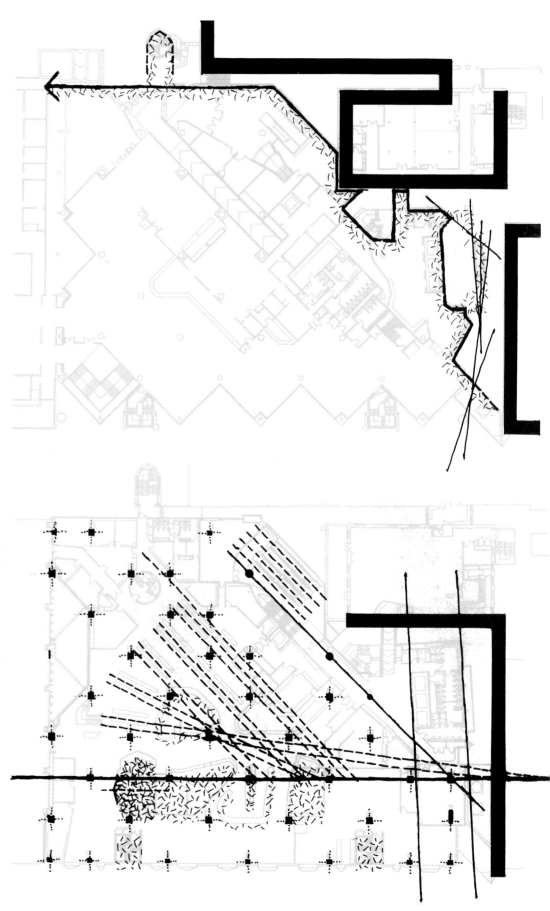

Level 4

This slight rotation also belongs to a meandering wall that outlines the side and back edge of the building, connecting Swanston Street and the edge of Building 10. This wall is full height, of one vertical piece at any one face and is just as variable as the spiral of columns under its south flanks.

Level 5

The diagonal grid is then ready to be brought back to the street. In the library, an open plan taking up the entire floor plate is established through a fan of shelves (and walls) that pull the diagonals of the Andrews columns around to set up a two-bay orthogonal street-related space filled with islands.

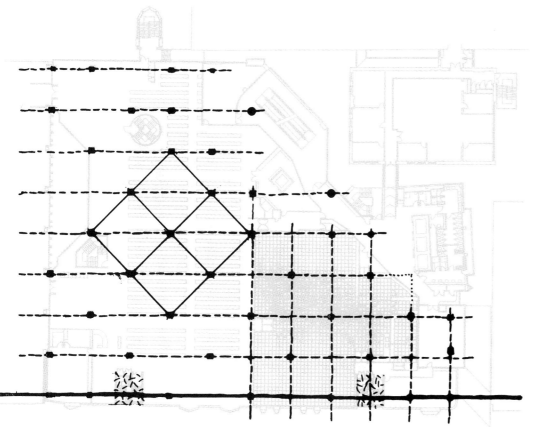

Level 6

At level 6, the stacks affirm the north-south lines of the columns, forming a smaller orthogonal grid connecting the diagonals of the diagonals. Meta-diagonals. The surroundings and the building grid have been pegged out, tamed, identified.

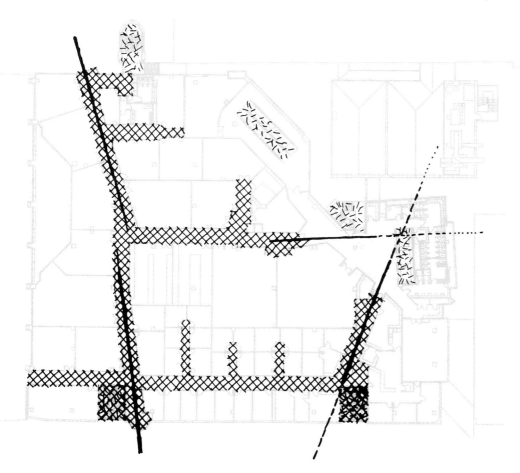

Level 7

From here on up, the building becomes a demonstration of urban, or rather, seeing this is Melbourne, suburban figures and models. At level 7 a road system is set out to begin the carve-up of the huge area of each floor plate. This system recognises the symmetrical dictum of the Swanston Street facade, but is bent, as real roads are, by local circumstances. It becomes, like many master plans, only partially realised.

Level 8

At level 8, the idea of
subdivision erupts as a
suburb of small blocks.
Each office is such a block,
with some of the blocks
retaining (as is the custom
or regulation) the
randomly-placed pre-
existing tree or column.
On this floor, the office
wall is the nine-to-five
paling fence.

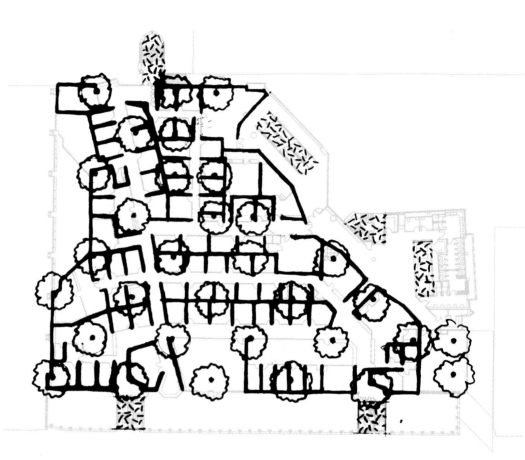

Level 9

One floor further up and
another suburban pattern
is deployed: zoning.
Recognisable through the
relative sizes of rooms,
there are zones of housing,
light industry, and heavy
industry. Note the
cul-de-sacs.

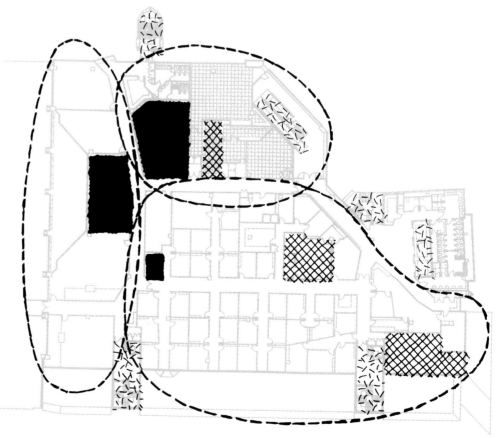

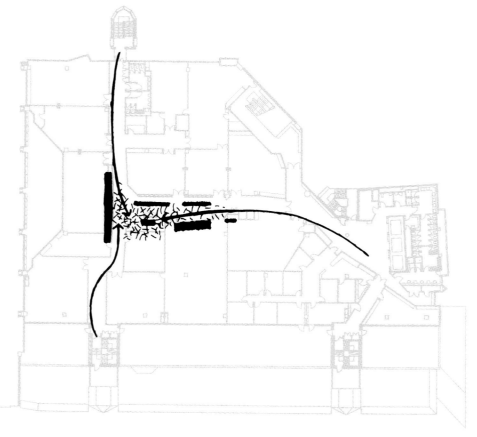

Level 10

Streets, blocks and zones
continue up the building.
But at level 10, the suburb
begins to develop formal
public places, expressions
of the polis. There is a
Shopping Street or rather,
Junction, with display
cases widening out into a
mall.

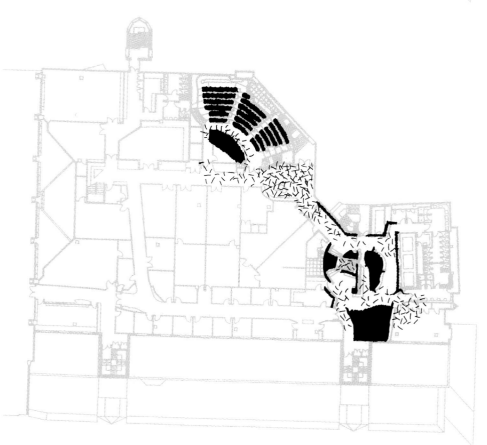

Level 11

On level 11, two theatres
anchor the south-east edge
of the floor. At the lifts a
dispersed modernist
theatre, deliberate in its
confusion (or
identification) of audience
and performer, stands
waiting for a new
production of Mother
Courage. Further over,
there is a traditional
theatre. Fixed seats radiate
around its fan shape and
the balcony seats hover
over a bio-box in which
the ghost of Don
Giovanni lurks.

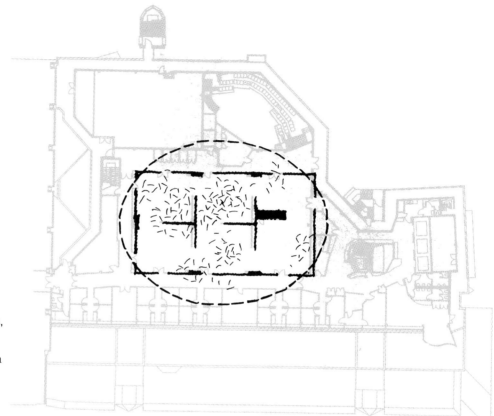

Level 12

On the ultimate floor, there is the ultimate space. Surrounded by a residential strip, the gods of the theatres and some heavy industry, there is a large inwardly-focussed arena. These atelier spaces, in which aspirations and native talent are tested, can be opened up into a larger field, into a virtual oval.

On Another Level

This fictional (or compositional) move up Building 8 is a progression from the relatively tangible geometries of the site, to planning strategies, to the modelling of symbolic spatial figures. Superficially, this is a movement from the literal to the metaphoric. In fact, the gestures at level 3 and 4 are just as metaphoric as those higher up, while the symbolic spaces at levels 9,10 and 11 are just as programmatic as those lower down. Further, all of the tropes unearthed in this narrative occur on every floor without exception, transformed, overlapping and bumping each other.

Finally, another fictional movement has to be identified, or admitted to, here. This set of drawings and its commentary is a reading of the building pulled apart in time to create a convincing narrative. It is not a description of how the architecture was made, of its real history or step-by-step realisation. But it is a fiction that permits one to scan the architecture. By denying the generalisation of this fiction, one can use it to begin a conversation which might discover the architecture that is there.

In this spirit, then, here is a conversation with two of the facades.

Bowen Lane

The meandering wall identified above as the third site-driven gesture of the composition is a facade where relatively little alters over its height. It is a figure most architects can recognise, an all-over surface of simple repeated elements. Its accompanying tower is a stack of identical elements, crowned with a band of something similar. What it says of the analysis offered above is "forget the imagery, the floors are basically the same".

Swanston Street

The Swanston Street facade has its towers too, but these are variegated: they change as they rise. At its base, each of the towers has a curved lump to take the compression of the big black struts. The concrete base is a conglomerate 1970s multilith. The passage up the building is then demonstrated in black granite; actually stairs, but disguised as a lift shaft complete with a giant ashtray and lights at each floor.

Alongside this shaft, the two library floors (the floors where the street geometry is re-established), can be identified by their light grey granite cladding. The library windows are golden cases, similar to the kind of cases that precious things are placed in.

Where the road system comes into existence, its junction with the wall is marked by a large bay window. The grey granite creeps halfway up this floor, rising as a tide line of knowledge.

Above the bay window, on the floor which reveals the paling fence, the repetitive pattern of this suburban figure is present in the loggia or pergola at the top of the facade on the street boundary.

At this point the facade recedes, isolating the two towers finished with cowls or masks which keep vigil over the zoning that begins in the floors inside. The facade itself is articulated with white pilasters, diamond windows and factory-like glazing, continuing the repetition suggested by the spirit of the paling fence.

In this zone, which in plan begins to solidify into images of the polis, one searches for and easily finds similar emblems grouped in a single view: the weather vane, signalling the sensitivity to slight changes in direction that characterises great politicians, the tapestry flag, and the military totems on the roof.

Mixed Metaphors

In this reading of the Swanston Street facade, a number of interpretations co-exist. The towers can be read as an architectural commentary on brutalism or Italian rationalism; bits of the facade can be seen in terms of their similarity to other built forms. Some parts are signs, like the bay window which stands for "street". Depending on the projections of the observer, bits can easily become metaphoric, as the level-by-level commentary demonstrates. All of these readings mix local, regional, national and international associations. In moving about this facade, one easily slips from sign to symbol, from fact to fiction, from one metaphor to another, from pure tectonics to representation, from one place to, sometimes it seems, just about everywhere. This makes the architecture like the piling up of different floor plates, which the building actually is — not a single metaphor of many meanings, but a simultaneous presence, or piling up, of similarity, of sign, symbol and metaphor.

Philip Goad

Architect as Editor as Author:
The Design Process of RMIT Building 8

This paper is an account from someone who worked in the office of Edmond & Corrigan from sketch design when the proposed extension to Building 8 was just a volumetric envelope, through to the day the tenders came in. It was exactly a year. There were a small number of us in the office. There were numbers after me. I was just part of an episode.

The paper, therefore, is part anecdotal, part chronicle, part speculation on aspects that I have assembled in retrospect, rather than what Maggie Edmond and Peter Corrigan might have intended for the building. It is not a blow-by-blow account of the design. The whole process was the sort of experience from which you invent your own stories.

In the beginning, there was the grim realisation of given physical rather than intellectual constraints. The fixed nature of the forty-five-degree diagonal column grid of John Andrews' existing Building 8 and an entry sequence that drew an indelible diagonal line across the site were compounded by the limits on vertical height due to the structural limitations of the existing building. Any extension would have to step back at the upper levels. To come to the street would require a massive brace or more columns. The floor levels of Bates Smart and McCutcheon's adjacent Building 10 were mean, low and architecturally naked — and connection had to be made through to them at every level. So there was a given vertical forest and a given stacking of horizontal plates. There were also burgeoning client requirements for accommodation where funding based on teaching and office space determined the maximisation of each floor plate. So the plan, by necessity, was deep. From the start, the interior was condemned to a state of perpetual gloom from which there would be no escape unless one went higher in the building.

With a series of client groups stacked vertically, each floor was to be its own labyrinth, its own city, harbouring its own dark and ironically bureaucratically cell-finding existence. As we in the office would develop rational plans, Corrigan would bend our straight corridors and twist them to become medieval streets in search of daylight, where bays would pop out of the skin, where paths would terminate at crossroads, the lift lobby, or a tiny hole from which to see the city and think of freedom. But these streets were made also to do what the Bates Smart and McCutcheon building was not — that is, to be unexpected, to be lost, to find one's way again, to find the edge and gain orientation, to be enlightened.

The building was thus constructed over the ruins of John Andrews' half-finished experiment in infinite adjustability and idealistic notions of flexible space planning. Instead of Andrews' open-ended matrix, Building 8 became specific, local and place-full. Corrigan was ever-mindful of the vitriol poured on the existing building by its vocal inhabitants. Instead of being open, universal and problem-solving in conception, Building 8 became building as castle, a bastion from which to look out on the city. In much the same way that the walled medieval city was in itself an expanded version of the castle, Building 8 quickly became

its own castellar fantasy with bridge connections to other buildings. It was parapeted, turreted and with its own gothic fancy work. As a building it was like Kandinsky's technicolour feats of expressionism that had embedded within them the romantic fables of St George and the dragon. Perhaps here was Corrigan's most evident attempt to engage with the spiritual and his oft-repeated phrase of "hope". Here was his answer to the Glass Chain's crystal cathedral — his apocalyptic answer to Melbourne's commercial towers and the dearth of any new institution within the city. Here was his other ideal. He had built his gritty temples for the people in the suburbs. Now it was time for the magic citadel, the urban fortress. This was an embattled institution, like some image from an Arthurian legend. It was definitely not to be the cosseted and accommodating monasticism of the university.

The building was thus peppered with its own fables and allusions. I was left a tiny palm-sized note scribbled in Biro and which depicted a patchwork of Texta colour and liquid paper with the words "Gothic vision/Albers" underneath. It was the single instruction to draw up the 7-storey glazed wall of the escalator lobbies — a chapel of movement to catch the eastern sun. The tacky columns with their mirrored surrounds in the library was described to me as "the magic forest". The button lights on Swanston street and the giant downpipes were "paste jewels". The window frames were to be "gold". Well, what else could they be, Philip? The hoods to the fire-escape stair exhausts were "Darth-vaders" or "Japanese warriors' masks". In Corrigan's quizzical style, this was to be a building of his own suggestion, but these clues were rarely instructions. They were descriptions which were scattered like flecks of mica through his conversations, overheard across the office or muttered during the intensely serious meetings at Demaine Partnership, where dreams became empirical and utterly professional, and the building entered the computers. As employees, one drew and built models, one coloured and re-coloured as the editorial additions and omissions breathed life into the rigorously consultative process of producing plans that functioned practically. Maggie Edmond orchestrated client briefing and her administrative net cast itself across the entire process, as below her mezzanine floor at Little La Trobe Street, we struggled to fit yet more space in after agonisingly long meetings about space and more space. Everyone wanted more. Throughout all that liaison and interpreting, it was the plans which the clients saw, not the concrete image of the bastion which was slowly rising on paper and in cardboard within the office.

Amid this private overlay of the castle and the organicism of the medieval city, there was a different cast of reference — an architecture of tribute that was both galactic and local. The bay windows of the library recalled Scarpa's windows on his bank in Verona (or was it Hollein's museum in Frankfurt or Stirling's building for Cornell?). Corrigan's books sometimes were laid like treasures before you on the drawing board. "Something like this"... the stair in Asplund's Gothenburg Town Hall extension "or this" ... Brancusi's sculpture in a garden in Rumania. There was Aalto's fan-shaped library and Kahn's stair cylinder from his Centre for British Art in New Haven. There was Kahn again in the served-and-servant spaces on the top floor of studios. There was Aalto's rustic Nordic siding in the cladding of the "Matterhorn" lift tower (or was it Erskine's pragmatic use of everyday materials as a gift of

texture and colour?). There were the Griffins' crystalline forms in the parapet, there was Stirling's polychromy and romantic functionalism in the Bowen Street stair tower. The front facade was a tribute to Venturi's decorated shed and an upturned finger to more tasteful composers within the town.

As a form of local tribute, the pale colours of the stained glass recalled more immediate tributes: the oculi of J.J. Clark's Federation Baroque City Baths. The tops of the stair towers at one point were to resemble the now lost zinc-tiled domes of the Queen Victoria Hospital. The facade was initially to be faced in bluestone and the parapet was to be copper, to age to green: Roy Grounds' gallery down the road and the Griffins' Newman College were to be connected at mid-point. The paste jewel lights and the giant rainwater heads and downpipes recalled Robert Haddon's Wharf Labourers Building; indeed, the whole building recalled the urban building designs in Haddon's text, Australian Architecture.[1] The polychromy of the stair tower facing Bowen Street was borrowed from the adjacent Percy Everett buildings with their dark brown bricks and resolutely horizontal bands. The interiors hailed football teams within the hallowed halls of education. These were interiors which you could hose down like the exteriors of Sydney watering holes. Handrails were to withstand the palms of thousands like well-worn communion rails. The bathrooms were shrines to tiling and colour like William Butterfield's increasing hierarchy of colour at St Paul's Cathedral down the road. But, of course, Butterfield's most heavily detailed and coloured piece was the altar, not, as in Building 8, where it occurred within the bathrooms. The curved burgundy corner was originally planned to be built of stone, like the beautiful bluestone corner detail of the nearby Carlton and United Brewery Building at Bouverie Street.

Corrigan's own descriptions of the building elements were more prosaic, Brechtian in their simplicity and bald commonness. The diagonal

[1] Robert Haddon, Architecture Australia, George Robertson, Melbourne, c. 1908.

struts which I primly thought of as references to Viollet-Le Duc or Guimard at Ecole Sacré-Coeur in Paris were described as "knitting needles", but were in fact detailed as if giant plumbing pipes; a sort of resourceful pragmatism and technological primitivism was applied rather than any chic high-tech solution. The metal siding of the service tower (a part of the building which itself was drawn over and over again as if revealing some obsessive preoccupation with the toilets and ducts) was referred to as the "garage doors". The drooping sprinkler heads in the light well were described as "Freudian" over the conference table. Edmond described one attempt at a street canopy as a "Hills-hoist". It disappeared overnight.

Throughout this process, the office became a studio. The double-height space of the Little La Trobe Street office became piled with cardboard models all of at least 1:50 scale. As the quantity of these grew, they began to be stored higher and higher in the office, concealing employees at their desk, as Corrigan himself would mooch between and ponder and discard and angrily ask another to be built. Things were never constant. The design was always to change. Above all, it was uncertain as to whether it would even stop. Hours were long, meetings with client groups in the office were detailed and painstaking. Meetings with consultants delved into minutiae and were also the encounters with the predictable petulance of the consultants: "Does he really want the wall to do that, or that bizarre lighting layout?" A whining "Why?" would always be the question. After a while, you just got used to it. The reward throughout the process might be Corrigan emerging with a recent purchase for his library, a giant illustrated folio of the contents of Chatsworth House, for example, which would then be whisked away back into the vaults of the front room of the office where the walls of books surrounded Corrigan deep in thought on his overstuffed black leather sofa.

Building 8 was not about purity of conception. Rather it was wild, untamed and unfettered by notions of civility. Yet surprisingly, the building sailed untouched through the planning process. It was pre-Renaissance in conception, of the nineteenth century in its vulgar Technicolour, definitively local in its hybrid assemblage of tributes which were then transformed to become a series of rich vignettes. Bridges connect old buildings; there are lanes and captured accidental views; there is a steel escape stair like a giant metal tree; and a skyline bristles like a bedecked castle with its crystal interior bulging over the top. There was Bruno Taut's alpine architecture as silhouette, white-capped and precipitous, and the stridency of the Gothic Revival on the street delivered as an untutored polychromatic rort. It was Venturi's signboard as the final tribute.

As with other buildings from the office, the use of client meetings, divergent staff skills, drawings and re-drawings, models and mock-ups, instruction and catechism — the observer is prodded out of complacency by the question — experiment and continual refinement are employed in the constantly shifting goal and the ever-becoming state of the editorial project. The result is the stage where finally the building takes on its own life and is ready to pass into the construction phase for yet another of its biographies. In all of this, the process had been a continual state of increasing territoriality as Corrigan's shifting opinions and experiment with the bits rather than the whole, and Edmond's criticism of her partner's sometimes fickle decisions, reached tension level yet again. In the end, we were not designing a building, we were designing someone's life.

Peter Kohane

Clothing the Institution

With its colourfully-clothed walls, polished jewellery-like adornments and sculptural roofscape, Edmond & Corrigan's RMIT Building 8 is an urbane and exciting addition to the public realm. Boldly raised above the three storeys of John Andrews' incomplete project of 1977-1983, it addresses both the spine of the RMIT campus along Bowen Street and Melbourne's main thoroughfare, Swanston Street, with appropriately chosen forms and materials. The Bowen Street facade is predominantly concrete, though enlivened with colourful tiles and a polychromatic brick stair tower. Nevertheless, when viewed in terms of the city, this is the building's back. The front — its facade, that is, its face, as well as its terraces — looks out onto Swanston Street and the city beyond. In keeping with this public function, forms are energetic and colourful. The facade is metaphorically a gateway, connecting and celebrating both city and institution. One could see the front as a theatre set, serving as a backdrop to an ideal urban life, its vibrant colours designed to contribute to the emotional and spiritual well-being of the city's inhabitants.

This essay focuses on the exterior of Building 8. Specifically, it explores those aspects of the building most accessible to public scrutiny, namely, the Swanston Street facade and the roofscape visible across the city. The design strategies Edmond & Corrigan employ to engage the attention and affections of the public will be analysed by referring to certain theories which have influenced architectural practice over several centuries. The most ancient and traditional of these is the analogy between architecture and the human form, clothed and adorned. Also important to an evaluation of the

1 Ducal Palace, Venice, fourteenth century (photo: author).

building is an understanding of the expressionist use of colour. I will argue that Edmond & Corrigan's Building 8 contributes to current architectural debates because it sustains interest in the power of built form to communicate with an audience of city dwellers.

The building's design acknowledges the cultural significance of Swanston Street as the city's major artery. Its extremities are defined by places of death and memory: to the north, Melbourne General Cemetery; to the south, the axial view of the Shrine of Rememberance. In between these two poles, the majority of the street's buildings — Carlton's orderly terrace houses and the city centre's bustling shops, banks and offices — shelter everyday activities. The long lines of their continuous facades create a backdrop against which many of the city's public institutions stand out in sharp relief. The symbolic centre of Melbourne is the Town Hall, defined by vigourously moulded walls, mansard roof, dramatic clock tower and monumental portico. Closer to RMIT, the State Library of Victoria and the Museum of Victoria is distinguished by a dignified and welcoming portico, while the Melbourne City Baths draws the eye with its striking contrast of red brick and white classical ornament. Just before the Yarra River, the boundary of the city grid is marked by the powerful massing and spires of St Paul's Cathedral. To judge ethically, these buildings turn their faces towards the public in a display of good manners; they do not neglect the street or turn their backs upon it, like some bad-mannered modern creations have a habit of doing.[1] A major achievement of Building 8 is that it sustains and reinterprets in a modern vein this ethical and rhetorical approach to architecture.

The RMIT campus is located within a dense pattern of streets. These provide a rich urban setting and potential source of inspiration for civic-minded design. Yet the possibilities of the site have frequently been ignored. Bates, Smart and McCutcheon's Casey Wing of 1967, for example, relies all too simply on its grand size and boldly articulated parts to express the importance of the institution and its position at a major juncture of Melbourne's grids. With its severe and inanimate forms the building is aristocratically divorced from the complex urban fabric and life that surrounds it. By contrast, in the new building Edmond & Corrigan employ structure, colour, cladding, attached ornaments and picturesque skyline to actively promote communication between the institution and the city, between the student inside and the public in the street. As with the Melbourne Town Hall or the State Library of Victoria and the Museum of Victoria, the building helps define the boundaries and cultural meaning of Swanston Street.

This kind of institutional and personal interaction is a social or political attribute effected through skillful design decisions. Principles of streetscape and contexturalism have informed the massing and ornament of Building 8. The Swanston Street facade respects the size of Storey Hall to the right, while the terraced masses behind elevate the building towards the Casey Building. This bridging function is reinforced in several ways. On the one hand, Storey Hall's classical entablature is reinterpreted to cap the facade of Building 8 with a colourful raked cornice, its frieze suggested by the colonnade of fins and the architrave by a black band below.[2]

[1] For a significant nineteenth-century contribution to this ethical reading of architecture, see E. L. Garbett, *Rudimentary Architecture for the Use of Beginners and Students. Principles of Design in Architecture, as Deducible from Nature, and Exemplified in the Works of the Greek and Gothic Architects*, 9th ed., Crosby, Lockwood & Son, London, 1908 (first published 1850), pp.1-30. For an analysis of Garbett's ideas, see P. Kohane, "Architecture, Labor and the Body: Fergusson, Cockerell and Ruskin", Doctorial dissertation, University of Pennsylvania, 1993, ch. 7, pp.227-44.

[2] This was more obviously an architrave in the narrower band shown in an earlier perspective. See C. Hamann, *Cities of Hope. Australian Architecture and Design by Edmond and Corrigan 1962-92*, Oxford University Press, Melbourne, 1993, fig. 246.

[3] The traditional analogy between architecture and the human body has its source in Vitruvius' restatement of the Polykleitan Canon. See Vitruvius, *On Architecture*, trans. F. Granger, 2 vols, Loeb Classical Library, Heinemann, London, 1931-34, p.251, 280; and G. Leftwich, "The Canon of Polykleitos: Tradition and Content", *Princeton Journal. Thematic Studies in Architecture 3: Canon*, 1988, pp.37-80.

[4] For a recent interpretation of monsters in architecture, see M. Frascari, *Monsters of Architecture. Anthropomorphism in Architectural Theory*, Rowan & Little, Savage, Maryland, 1991.

[5] As pointed out by Philip Goad. See Hamann, op cit, p.146.

[6] Published in E.-E. Viollet-le-Duc, *Lectures*

2 Hector Guimard, Ecole du Sacré Coeur, Paris, 1895 (photo: Philip Goad).

3 Eugène Emmanuel Viollet-le-Duc, project for a Market Hall. Source: E.-E. Viollet-le-Duc, *Lectures on Architecture*, trans. B. Bucknall, Dover, London, [reprint of 1877 and 1881 English edition, first published in french, 1863-72], vol. 2, pl. XXI.

4 Gottfried Semper, Carribean hut. Source: G. Semper, *Der Stil in Technishen und Tektonischen Künsten, oder Praktische Aesthetik*, vol. 2, Friedrich Bruckmann, Munich, 1863

5 Paul Klee, "The Acrobat", 1930 (photo: M. Plant, *Paul Klee, Figures and Faces*, Thames & Hudson, London, 1978, pl. XXIII).

6 Edmond and Corrigan, Tony Lockett ("Plugger") collage for display at the 1991 Venice Biennale.

On the other hand, the Casey Building's massing, with its two major projecting towers separating three horizontal parts, is echoed in Building 8's horizontal organisation, broken by two rising, but now recessed, black stair towers. In this way, Edmond & Corrigan's design incorporates themes from its Swanston Street neighbours. Supported on its black pipe trusses, the new building is a literal bridge between the earlier structures, joining them together as it passes above Andrews' building.

Building 8 can also be seen metaphorically as a body. This is not, however, the harmoniously proportioned human body of traditional classical theory.[3] Rather, Edmond & Corrigan have delighted in fashioning an imperfect creature, a monster,[4] the bizarre outcome of two quite distinct building campaigns by two separate architectural firms, motivated by radically different design philosophies. Below, Andrews' earlier building boldly reveals its concrete structure: the floor slabs and cylindrical columns visibly carry loads to the ground. Within this sturdy frame is inset the glazed, non-structural wall. Above, Edmond & Corrigan's building hides its concrete structure behind a flat surface, a cladding into which windows are cut. The structural members are only revealed at the lower levels, that is, those initially designed by Andrews.

Quite self-consciously, Edmond & Corrigan complement the muscular structure of the earlier building with a flamboyant truss, the two diagonal members of which rise dramatically out of the powerful concrete bases of the stair towers. This metal structure is explicitly derived from a building by the famous Art Nouveau architect Hector Guimard, the Ecole du Sacré Coeur in Paris (1895) (fig. 2)[5] as well as from Guimard's own source, projects such as the Market Hall (circa 1863) by the Gothic Revival architect Eugène Emmanuel Viollet-le-Duc (fig. 3).[6] With this quotation Edmond & Corrigan historicise and contexturalise Andrews' structuralist approach, locating it within the continuing tradition of French rationalism. Modern scholars have dubbed this approach the "Graeco-Gothic ideal", because its principles were initially derived from eighteenth- and nineteenth-century scientific analyses of Greek and Gothic structure.[7] In this tradition, structural members have often been likened to the members of a body. Viollet-le-Duc, for instance, made drawings of the human skeleton to guide structural design, and identified an elastic, human-like attribute in structure. The concrete construction of Andrews' building and that of metal in Edmond & Corrigan's are linked in that they are taut and muscular, exhibiting a human-like vitality and energy. Informed by French rationalism, both structural systems are clearly stated to convey immediately the sensation of bodily weight and presence.

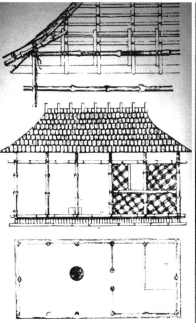

GOTTFRIED SEMPER *Der Stil vol 2 page 263* Caraib hut

Above this structural level is the colourfully-patterned facade, a dressing or clothing of the underlying naked structure. This method of treating the surface draws on an analogy between dressing the wall and the body, most imaginatively explored in the writings of the nineteenth-century architect and theorist Gottfried Semper.[8] For Semper, the significance of the wall could be fathomed by reflecting on its source in the craft of weaving and the making of fabrics (fig. 4). He invoked the architectural principle of "material transformation" to explain the historical substitution of the original woven wall for its imitation, a more permanent dressing exhibiting weaving patterns. This is now the ornament of a monumental work of architecture. In this way, Semper related clothing the body in fabrics to clothing a building's structure with ornament metaphorically referring to the craft of weaving.

Edmond & Corrigan's ornamental cladding has weaving patterns to enhance the building's role as a theatrical backdrop for urban life. Splendidly dressed, Building 8 contributes to the drama of the street, conceived as a place where equally well-dressed citizens perform like actors on a stage.[9] One can pursue the analogy even further, envisaging architecture as a person bedecked with jewellery to complement his or her fine clothes. Thus, Building 8 has a cloth-like surface as well as red and gold window frames, down pipes with

conical sumps, and silver bolts and lighting fixtures. Suitably dressed and adorned, the building appears as a bodily presence. The two revealed structural systems of the lowest levels are like muscular legs, vigorously supporting the storeys above. This upper surface becomes a torso, with its heads as the silver, Gaudi-like[10] tops of the two stair towers. The gold louvres are glasses shielding eyes which confidently survey the surrounding city. Such architectural anthropomorphism may have been shaped by Corrigan's enthusiasm for early twentieth-century European art. In particular, the squat shape of Building 8 surmounting spread-eagled legs recalls the thin-legged and wide-torsoed figure encountered in the work of Paul Klee from the 1920s (fig. 5).[11]

The vivid colouring of the design invites one to identify this bodily representation even more specifically, as a football player (Australian Rules, of course). References to that quintessential Australian game abound in the works of Edmond & Corrigan, including a collage the firm displayed at the 1991 Venice Biennale (fig. 6).[12] The same dynamic energy captured in the photograph can also be recognised in the RMIT building, with its diagonal truss members leaping from their angled concrete base and the vibrant, colourful football guernsey above.

on Architecture, trans. B. Bucknall, Dover, London [reprint of 1877 and 1881 English editions, first published in French, 1863-72], Vol. II, pl. XXI.

[7] *See R.D. Middleton and D. Watkin, Neoclassical and 19th Century Architecture, Electa/Rizzoli, New York, 1980, Vol. I, pp.7-34.*

[8] *See G. Semper, The Four Elements of Architecture and Other Writings, trans. H.F. Mallgrave and W. Herrmann, intro. H.F. Mallgrave, Cambridge University Press, Cambridge, 1989 (first published 1851). Semper's ideas on clothing and weaving are analysed in W. Herrmann, Gottfried Semper. In Search of Architecture, MIT Press, Cambridge, Mass., 1984; and J. Rykwert, "Semper and the Conception of Style", in his The Necessity of Artifice, Rizzoli, New York, 1982, pp.123-30.*

[9] *For Corrigan's theatre work, see M.A.R. Anderson, "Pressing against Ideas", in Hamann, op cit, pp.149-58.*

[10] *Edmond & Corrigan's design of the heads was probably inspired by the mask-like forms on the roof of Antonio Gaudi's Casa Mila, Barcelona, 1905-10. On Corrigan's admiration for Gaudi, see his comments in an interview with Peter Hyatt, "Prince of Shadows: Prince of Light", reprinted in Vol. 3 of this edition, The Writings of Edmond and Corrigan.*

54

7a Ionic column, the Erechtheion, the Acropolis, Athens, 421-405 B.C. (photo: author).

7b Detail of drapery and sandals of Greek kore (Istanbul, Archaeological Museum) (photo: author).

However, this interpretation will not convince those who know that real footballers do not wear jewellery. An alternative gendered reading can be offered by considering the design in terms of the traditional conception of the classical orders, particularly the female Ionic column.[13] It is apparent that the firm of Edmond & Corrigan is not interested in the conventional role of the orders in establishing the proportions of an entire building. Free of the classical dictum which decrees that each part of the building be related to each other and to the whole, the architects can abruptly juxtapose the concrete levels of Andrews' structure with their own dressed facade above. Nevertheless, some reference to the classical orders remains.

In ancient Greek sculpture, nudity was reserved for the male form, while women were generally represented wearing drapery and sandals.[14] It is this clothed and shod female form which is invoked in the Ionic column, its fluting gracefully folding up over a moulded base like the fall of a garment over a shoe (figs. 7a, 7b). The multi-coloured, dress-like stone surface of Building 8's facade recalls the fluting of the Ionic column. Both column and building are stone imitations of clothing worn by a human being. In Edmond & Corrigan's facade, however, the drapery does not fall to lap over

sandalled feet, but is raised above naked legs. Such nudity is a breach of decorum in classical terms, but here enables both male and female readings of the clothed architectural body. It thus seems to me that the issue of dressing and "material transformation", so important in ancient architecture, is a key element in the building's appeal, which serves to enhance a sense of charged communication between the bodies of architecture and of human beings.

The architects' interest in fostering connections between building and inhabitants is also effected by oriel windows. These link the more public interior spaces with the street. For example, the sitting area at the end of a corridor on level 7 is extended beyond the facade to become a large red oriel, while the two levels of the open-planned library below are characterised by an array of projecting windows. In terms of the facade composition, the oriels connect different levels by restating the form of the heads of the stair towers. It is an appropriate conjunction, since both shapes have bodily resonances: the tops of the towers look like silver heads, complete with eyes, while the oriel windows actually function as eyes. This is made abundantly clear by the paired windows on the upper library level, which inevitably read as black eyebrows above the oriel eyes.

As eyes, the oriel windows peer out in various directions. Looking with their own eyes, staff and students within the building have their gazes framed by the windows. A view through the red oriel specifically directs attention at A'Beckett Street as it runs west, away from Swanston Street below. The most important oriels look south along Swanston Street, taking in the Town Hall, St Paul's Cathedral and the Shrine of Remembrance. Here, the act of seeing inspires reflection, allowing the observer to consider his or her relationship with an array of political, religious and cultural values, past and present.

While the windows look outward, they also project to meet the gaze of those looking from the city below. Again, the building promotes interaction with the public. From the street, one's attention is drawn to the building's sparkling eyes, making it not just a well-dressed creature, but one with a vivacious personality.[15] This social relationship between those within the building and the public without could have been further dramatised by the eighth floor roof terrace looking over Swanston Street. Like the oriel windows, this offers views across the city. Yet, unfortunately, the terrace's parapet wall is high and difficult to look over. One can see, but cannot be seen from, the street. Thus, although the building has the quality of a theatrical set, here an opportunity to animate it with actors, staff and students enjoying their leisure high above the street, is neglected.

The trabeated colonnade of the roof terrace is the building's freize and cornice, capping the two lower elements of Andrews' structure and Edmond & Corrigan's facade. The uppermost section of the building, containing three floors and mechanical services such as the lift machinery, rises in powerful masses from the roof-garden level. Viewed from the street below, these stepped-back forms are appropriately unobtrusive. From afar, however, particularly from the south, they appear as a series of sharply defined masses, a colourful mountain dramatically set against the city and sky. This roofscape complements both the well-dressed facade with

its oriel window-eyes and the robust supporting legs in representing the institution to city dwellers. Readable at different scales, the legs, facade and sculpted top all contribute to isolate the building from its urban context of generally banal buildings. The deliberate sense of contrast is equally evident in the way the building has incorporated formal themes from its immediate neighbours while dramatically distinguishing itself with colour and a vibrant composition of parts. Edmond & Corrigan has taken a prophetic role, providing Melburnians with a glimpse of an alternative architecture, city and life.

I see Building 8 as intended to stimulate wonder, perhaps even spiritual insight. In a recent interview, Peter Corrigan mentioned how much he liked Howard Raggatt's interpretation of the building as "a fragment of the wall of the new city of Jerusalem".[16] This refers to the heavenly paradise of the New Jerusalem in which the just will reign forever with Christ at the end of time, as described in the Book of Revelations (Rev. 21:19-20). The Biblical image is of a twelve-gated city encircled by a high wall, set with precious stones.[17] With this reference in mind, Edmond & Corrigan's facade can be seen as the segment of a wall surrounding RMIT, a modern institution transformed into a paradisal city of learning and spiritual understanding. Reinforcing this interpretation is the distant view: Building 8's masses rise from behind its wall-like facade, invoking descriptions of paradise as a terraced mountain. This imagery informed projects well known to Edmond & Corrigan, including Gaudi's Park Güell and Bruno Taut's expressionist schemes with crystals, mountains and stepped pyramids (fig. 8).[18]

Corrigan's interest in the New Jerusalem might suggest another level of meaning for the colour in Building 8. Many modern artists and theorists have argued for the charged

[11] I am grateful to Philip Goad, who worked on the project for Building 8, for his verbal confirmation of Corrigan's interest in artists such as Klee and Wassily Kandinsky. It is worth noting that Edmond & Corrigan designed a home for Margaret Plant, Professor of the Department of Visual Arts at Monash University and author of an important study of Klee's paintings of the human figure: Paul Klee, Figures and Faces, Thames and Hudson, London, 1978. Plant's study includes several Klee paintings that may have informed the design for Building 8, including "Equilibrist", 1923; "Fool in a Trance", 1929; "Acrobat", 1930; and "Allegorical Figure", 1927. See pls.XI, XIV and XXIII and fig. 74. For Edmond & Corrigan's Plant house design, see Hamann, op cit, p.125.

[12] On this project, see Hamann, op cit, pp.110-11.

[13] On the classical theory of the orders, see Vitruvius; and J. Rykwert, "Body and Building", Daidalos, 15, 1992, pp.100-09.

[14] See Ibid.

[15] For a valuable study of nineteenth-century theories of architecture's creaturely quality, see G.L. Hersey, High Victorian Gothic. A Study in Associationism, The Johns Hopkins University Press, Baltimore, 1972. His analysis of windows in terms of the expression of human characteristics is relevant to Building 8: see Hersey, op cit, pp.25-9.

[16] Interview with Peter Hyatt, loc cit.

[17] Corrigan may have also known of the description of the city of Ecabanta in Herodotus, where the colourful walls were interpreted as a defensive charm. This was relevant to the analysis of Henri Labrouste's "Agrigentum" drawing, which was surely considered by Corrigan's history teachers at Yale. See P. Kohane, "Everyday Life and Architectural Polychromy: Romanticism and the Buildings of Edmond & Corrigan", this volume.

[18] For the terraced paradisal mountain in Gaudi, see C. Kent and D. Prindle, Park Güell, Princeton Architectural Press, Princeton, pp.189-90. On German expressionist architecture,

8. Bruno Taut, Crystal Mountain project (from B. Taut, *Alpine Architektur*, 1919; Source: W. Curtis, *Modern Architecture since 1900*, 2nd ed., Phaidon, Oxford, 1989, fig. 9.1).

9. Wassily Kandinsky, "Riding Couple", 1906-7 (Munich, Städtische Galerie im Lenbachhaus) (photo: H. Düchting, *Wassily Kandinsky, 1866-1944. A Revolution in Painting*, Taschen, Cologne, 1991, p. 6).

see K. Frampton, *Modern Architecture. A Critical History*, Thames & Hudson, London, 1980, pp.116-22; and W. Curtis, *Modern Architecture since 1900*, 2nd ed., Phaidon, Oxford, 1987, pp.118-19, and fig. 9.1, illustrating Bruno Taut's "Crystal Mountain" project from his book *Alpine Architektur*, 1919. Corrigan's interest in German expressionism and the work of architects like Bruno Taut was related to me by Philip Goad.

[19] See W. Kandinsky, *Concerning the Spiritual in Art*, Wittenborn, New York, 1955 (first published 1912).

[20] Verbal communication, Philip Goad.

[21] These buildings are discussed and illustrated in Hamann, op cit, pp.50-74.

[22] For a discussion of this topic, see P. Kohane, "Architecture, Labor and the Body: Fergusson, Cockerell and Ruskin", pp. 423-30; and J. Unrau, *Looking at Architecture with Ruskin*, Thames and Hudson, London, 1978, pp.51-64.

[23] A famous example is "Riding Couple", 1906-7 (Lenbachhaus,Munich).

[24] Interview with Peter Hyatt, loc cit.

significance of colour. One of the most profound is the painter Wassily Kandinsky, in his book Concerning the Spiritual in Art (1912).[19] Corrigan admires Kandinsky and has encouraged his architecture students to investigate the artist's works.[20] For Kandinsky, intensely coloured abstract forms in painting encouraged viewers to see beyond the mere materiality of things and experience their "inner necessity". Such heightened perception foreshadowed the "new spiritual epoch", a world which would replace the materialist one in the aftermath of the apocalypse.

While Edmond & Corrigan may not share Kandinsky's enthusiasm for the end of this world, they would admire his theory of colour, particularly the explanation of its almost occult power to communicate immediately with the beholder. This notion is especially relevant to Building 8. In Edmond & Corrigan's earlier buildings, such as those at Keysborough and Box Hill, colours and particular forms were chosen to establish associational connections with the surrounding architectural fabric.[21] A very different cultural strategy has been explored at RMIT, where colour strongly distinguishes Building 8 from its urban setting. This building relies on the expressionist belief in the capacity of colour to engage the viewer directly, unmediated by specific references or symbols. Although some observers could recognise local associations with football guernseys, all could enjoy the emotional and spiritual qualities of the colours.

A suggestion of movement in formal relationships reinforces the direct appeal of colour to an audience's sensibilities. This conjunction can be seen in various guises. On the Swanston Street facade, the contrasting black and grey stone surfaces provide a relatively sedate setting for a lively, staccato play of gold and red windows, green and red inset panels and various silver adornments. Colour and movement also characterise both the metal-clad south front and the roofscape, with its brightly coloured elements such as the tiled, flag-shaped meeting room.

A more subtle interpretation of this theme is the arrangement of the simple gold windows running across the facade above the library levels. The constant shifting in spacing is comparable to the endlessly varied inter-columniations found in the medieval architecture of Tuscany and Venice. In this respect, Edmond & Corrigan could have been influenced by the widely-read nineteenth-century architecture critic John Ruskin, who was a vehement defender of medieval architecture. Ruskin carefully measured Italian Romanesque buildings such as the Cathedral of Pisa to demonstrate the ways in which they exhibited a vital and organic, rather than mechanical, symmetry.[22] In his view, this was a higher level of symmetry which connected built form with the changeability and beauty of God's nature, as instanced in clouds or mountains. For Ruskin, as well as Kandinsky, colour and movement of form inspired insight into the divine in nature.

The new RMIT building can also be linked to Ruskin and Kandinsky in their admiration for medieval cities as guides in the definition of an ideal architecture. Like Ruskin and Kandinsky, the firm of Edmond & Corrigan is critical of the modern city, its blandness deemed an inadequate representation of human potential. All these critics develop alternatives by interpreting past architecture and visionary texts. Ruskin looked back to the Middle Ages, often focusing on Venice. In the first decade of this century, Kandinsky painted imaginary cities where buildings and citizens alike are clothed in bright colours and adornments (fig. 9).[23] Evidently his utopia belonged as much to the Middle Ages as to the post-apocalyptic "new spiritual epoch".

The imagery of Edmond & Corrigan's post-apocalyptic city, the New Jerusalem, is likewise inspired by the medieval city. Indeed, Corrigan's comment regarding the New Jerusalem was followed by a reference to his building as composed of "contextual dreams, memories, reminiscences, smudges and shadings that cross the face of the building. It's a tangled medieval dream

— not exactly Hobbitesque — but it's a romantic construction...".[24] One of the most evocative sources for such a romantic dream of a visionary city appears to have been medieval Venice, especially the Ducal Palace (fig. 1). Both this Venetian example and Building 8 have strong columns articulating lower levels and a colourful, tapestry-like wall above, which Ruskin aptly termed the "wall-veil". The dressing metaphor is, as we have seen, particularly relevant to the RMIT building, whose architects could have admired the Ducal Palace for its scenographic qualities, for the way it functions as an appropriately sumptuous and colourful representation of prevailing communal and religious values.

Such an interpretation of medieval architecture and life connects Edmond & Corrigan to a critical cultural tradition which was elaborated in nineteenth-century Britain. Writers such as Thomas Carlyle and Ruskin attacked modern British society for its relentless pursuit of industrialism and capitalism, eradicating a richer communal life in the process. Indebted to this ethical critique, Edmond & Corrigan's earlier work has consistently sought to oppose prevailing utilitarian values and the concomitant stultifying dullness of the modern city. At Keysborough, their approach has been to employ symbols whose meanings are clearly understood by the building's users and to unite them in community. By contrast, Building 8 is less concerned with this explicit connection between community and contextual form. The architects have enthusiastically embraced more remote sources of inspiration, such as medieval buildings. Nevertheless, the critical function of architecture remains. At RMIT, the firm of Edmond & Corrigan has designed a building with strong legs, colourful clothing and sparkling, eye-like windows to capture the attention of city-dwellers, offering them a vision of a more vibrant, rhetorical and spritual life. Respecting the theoretical relationship between decoration and decorum, the building has been conceived in terms of a social transaction, an appropriately ornate gift from RMIT to the community of citizens.

Jennifer Hocking

Building as Event:
An Eruption from the Crypt of Modernity

Preface

As an independent reading of an architectural object, this paper in no way seeks to suggest the manner in which the architects Edmond & Corrigan may have approached the design of this building. Rather, the intention is to discuss and reflect upon some of the conditions in which contemporary architecture and spatial urban conditions may be created and read. This is not about seeking one "truth" for the architectural object; rather, it is about seeing architecture as a provocative source of discussion.

Context

To set the scene for this dialogue I would like to make a few observations regarding the modern condition of architecture within which, both conceptually and physically, John Andrews' Union Building was constructed, and with which Edmond & Corrigan's building works.

Predicated upon the notion of there being essential criteria upon which various aesthetic decisions could be based, modernism not only partook of a search for these states of purity and honesty underlying the objects it spawned, a search of proportions not unlike the quest for the Holy Grail, but also even before this constructed the very desire for these criteria.

Among other things modernism articulated and constructed was the split between ornament and structure, art and architecture, taste and consumption.[1] Modernism had to perform the most violent acts of repression in order to maintain such dialectically pure polarities. These could not, however, be sustained. The totalitarian utopian dream of modernism was inevitably to fail with the emergence of numerous local and global economies constituted by cultural, gender,

class and racial differences, the very sites repressed but not erased by such a hegemonic system. With the recognition of the value of differences engendered in marginalised groups arose the space of a post-colonialist debate which valued multiplicity, a discourse which was intent on recognising different voices and interpretations, different ways of seeing and operating in the world. During the past few decades the urban Australian condition in the architectural arena could be seen to be one of these minority spaces struggling to establish its own language, a distortion of the European and American models it had inherited. The totalitarian model was seen to fall under inconsistent pressures and forces, in response to different desires. Cracks not only began to appear on the surface but, more radically, were recognised as always having been present in the foundations upon which modernism had been constructed.[2]

These events brought with them the ability to realise that the inevitable and inherent points of failure of any system are already contained within it. Therefore, to challenge and extend, alter or amend any system to accommodate or recognise excluded dialogues or spaces one should act from within. So to challenge the limitations of the modernist dialogue, to move beyond it rather than merely overthrow one exclusivist, repressive system for yet another, the answering action may be to continue to work with it rather than deny it. Once modernist dialectical opposites are realised as being of limited value one's course of action is not merely about moving back into a prior system of order to compensate. Neither is it simply about a mere inversion of these polarities. Rather, each proposed framework for action is now defined within an ongoing, always shifting and conditional reading and experience of architecture.

Photo: author.

Multiple new allegiances are now able to be proposed and perceived, ones which require constant re-definition, reconstructing themselves with each event.

If Andrews' building is representative of the modernist dialogue, I propose Edmond & Corrigan's building as being representative of that which flows out of the violent repression caused by the modernist condition. It is an extension, not a replacement, of this framework, working with urban spatial complexities, not erasing them.

The new allegiances which Edmond & Corrigan's Building 8 marks muddies the space and language of Andrews' Union Building, yet leaves enough of it to produce an architecture intent on the maintenance of "difference" articulating a space between any totalitarian actions.

The Act/Event of Building 8

Edmond & Corrigan's Building 8 can be said to drape, settle upon, or build over Andrews' Union Building. I, however, would prefer to describe the event of Building 8 to be more about the acts of swallowing, ingesting, and consuming, not as total and easy actions, but as emotive terms descriptive of unease and incompleteness. Building 8 raises its skirts to expose a dialogue with the Union Building, to establish its otherness of colour, ornament and quotation against the mute glass block walls of the Andrews' building. This action of partial exposure at once both establishes and sustains Building 8's formal position.

The modern brutalism of the Andrews' building represents — and indeed displays a desire most strongly for — a modernist rationality evident in the apparent divorcing of ornament from structure,

in its denial of the use of a facade (in the classical sense), and in its preference for the "honesty" of structure and "truth" to materials of high modernism. It is also decidedly inarticulate with reference to the street, to the point of perpetrating an active and violent exclusion of any internal/external dialogue. This is further clarified when it is juxtaposed with the resource-intense facade of Building 8 which sets up and focuses its actions upon an urban dialogue.

Within the modern context of dialectical oppositions, Edmond & Corrigan's building can be seen as the antithesis of Andrews' Union Building. Yet, I would pro-offer Building 8 as not only being this, but also acting as an extension to it, depending upon, yet moving literally beyond/over/out from, the limits of a modern piece of architecture. I call Building 8 an "event" because here we have a piece of architecture which cannot only be conceptually located in this discourse, but is one which quite literally acts out the discourse.

As an antithesis to the Union Building with its mute, monotonous, scaleless facade, Building 8 uses ornament as a language of the city which allows the observer, or user, of the building a personal involvement. It allows the individual the chance to read personally and interpret their own narrative in the facade. The colour, elaborate detailing, multiple surface treatments, different window shapes, all these evoke certain memories, recall other city objects, (mis)quote other icons and generally possess a sense of humour and wit. It appeals to our emotions. Building 8 inherently desires to communicate with the streetscape and, in this manner, in contradistinction to the modern object it operates with, it can be termed grotesque.

[1] Mark Wigley, "Postmodern Architecture: The Taste of Derrida", Perspecta 23, 1987, pp.156-72.

[2] Ibid.

[3] "RMIT Student Union", Constructional Review, May 1983, p.35. See also Nigel Bertram, "Institutional Imagings: Site and Desire in Swanston Street", this volume (ed.).

The Violence of the Union Building

The modernist architect's attitude towards colour, ornament and texture was to subordinate them to formal structural design issues, if not suppress them completely. Such embellishments in modernism were generally marginalised as design elements. They were allied to a state of primitivism, as evidenced in the texts of such modern architects as Loos, Le Corbusier, and Mies van der Rohe or, in the local context, Robin Boyd. These haptic elements were seen as being "*purely (about) a pleasure of the senses*", the use of which was evidence of the designer operating from a primitive emotive condition rather than being concerned with demonstrating the higher, yet paradoxically more fundamental, truth of an honesty to materials, a truth of form fitting function, and a clarity of formal purpose to the eye. The preoccupation with these aspects of making space and form demonstrated a desire for a reasoned and sophisticated position, but were not necessarily a statement of having obtained such a position.

Colour, particularly when used as ornament, was not held worthy of serious architectural consideration in a contemporary sophisticated modern society, a society far removed from such acts of barbarism as tattooing, colouring-in, decorating, or even displaying a sense of humour. These elements, if used at all, were allocated to the formal margins of architecture, as was to be seen in the detailing of a feature wall, the colouring of window trims or glazed transom panels. These elements were contained, framed and limited, to be used only when under knowledgeable control.

The brutalism of Andrews' Union Building is an excellent example of this position, as it possesses no colour or ornament, desires no haptic interaction with the observer at all and indeed displays an active will to exclude the observer, reducing our involvement to one of purely optic reference.

In a contemporary critique it was claimed that the use of glass bricks in the Union Building made the "shimmer of movement of people inside ... visible to the passers by day and night, whilst the users (were) aware of the city outside but (were) protected from the high noise levels of Swanston Street".[3] In fact the glass blocks severed the interior from the exterior. The interior was an independent and isolated space with little if any relationship to its urban condition. Instead, a tenuous and ambiguous translucency existed, offering neither transparent visual connections to the exterior, nor physically direct points of penetration. There were not even any implied points of contact via surface articulation, and little connection via surface animation or reflection. Once within the old Union Building one suffered an acute separation from the urban environment one had just come from, and this was compounded by the act of the building's orthogonal forty-five degree rotational shift where a full re-orientation occurred. Upon entry and re-emergence from this internalised and "other" environment, the city is presented as an "other" world, disconnected and disconnecting.

The glass block exterior walls remained mute and unreceptive to both internal and external conditions. Acting as a shard of opacity slicing off space more effectively than an articulated solid masonry wall could, the glass block walls carried with them the illusion, the promise of transparency which, despite this promise, violently prevented it from happening. These walls acted as screens, impenetrable boundaries, edges with little dialogue between the two spaces.

With the construction of Edmond & Corrigan's Building 8, however, ornament, colour, quotations, reflections, and surface punctuations make the building move into the chaotic language of the street and comfort us with its presence. It seems to preen itself in public, arguing and elbowing its way into our line of vision. It appears to erupt from a space formerly hidden within and concealed by the silent form of modernity.

Photographs: author.

An Eruption from the Crypt of Modernity

In its eruption from the Union Building (and also perhaps from the adjacent buildings by Bates Smart & McCutcheon), Building 8 relies on memory and repressed emotions once allied with the qualities and elements of architecture which these modern buildings deny. It evokes qualities which were formerly associated with frivolous, primitive and wilful images, which in the contemporary condition creates a certain state of unheimlich, a certain uncanny evocation of what is familiar but no longer clearly understood because of its many years of denial.

Building 8 brings to the surface, through such elements as ornament, colour, and humour, the grotesque which had been suppressed by the silence of Andrews' Union Building. In so doing, it generates strong responses, and, often for those not prepared to admit the limits of modernism, feelings of disgust. It represents that which modernism could not digest, could not quite consume and which modernism had attempted to keep hidden. Here it is all regurgitated onto the surface.

The modernist desire to sever bodily attachment to the object, to detach all desires, all interest from the object, is evidenced par excellence in Andrews' Union Building. In the ultimate realisation of a modern city, most clearly to be read in the projects of Hilberseimer, we could not afford to associate the lost modernist object with the loss of ourselves in the utopian monologue of modernism. A necessary disassociation had to occur between the body and the object, or we would ourselves be as silent as these buildings.

With Edmond & Corrigan's building we see our attachment re-established not only in a classical manner via the surface dialogue of the facade, but also through the upwards movement of the building itself, as evidenced in the public circulation spaces.

Yet, Building 8 also keeps Andrews' building as other, as foreign within itself and contains it without being contaminated by it. It thereby prevents a mere inversion of one order by another and prevents an equivalent state of ennui from developing, prevents a horreur vacuui of ornament, of the grotesque.

Building 8 does not commit the same purist act as Andrews' Union Building, for it has learnt not to seek to consume that which it realises it can never fully digest. It does not necessitate the establishment of the crypt to keep modernism secretly contained and undigested. modernism is not sequestered to be regurgitated at another time; it is presenced and recognised, perhaps preventing it from being consumed in the future by that which it keeps hidden in its own crypt.

But then perhaps I cannot yet see what is kept in Building 8's crypt, the act of encrypting necessarily being something to which I cannot at the moment gain access, something which may only be deciphered over time. Some other event may well consume Edmond & Corrigan's Building 8 but it will not be the same action that gave rise to it. Building 8 allows recognition of its "other" in Andrews' building, thereby strengthening itself and its actions in doing so. It does not need to encrypt anything, or to suggest the concealment of a deeper truth.

Andrews' Union Building desired to express the clarity and purity of a singular truth, necessitating a silencing of potentially undermining moments of doubt or the existence of other possible interactions with it, keeping them encrypted, distanced, unobtainable, separate. Building 8, which includes the preservation of moments of the Union Building, thrives on ambiguity, the surprise, the "incorrect" reading, the creation of a new joke, the missing punchline created by your presence and perception.

Craig Bremner

Written on the Building: Patterns of Projection from Building 8

The patterns which guide our movements through the metropolitan landscape are complex and contradictory. The source of these patterns is increasingly the universal flow of information which spins around us, and the way in which it guides us is an affair which mixes seduction with betrayal. On the one hand, we are seduced by these universal patterns we read in the images of landscapes transmitted from elsewhere while, on the other hand, when trying to translate them here, they betray us by the absence of the advice, the suggestions and the handy hints, the anecdotes.

In the absence of the background to these pictures the patterns can only present universal models. These universal models then have to be made real by the anecdotes which, in their place of origin, would bring back memories and inspire recognition of the world-as-found — ie, fill in the picture. Anecdotes transform the universal models into instances of the present state of affairs; they are the temporary form of the patterns, just as the patterns are the comprehensive form of all anecdotes.

Therefore, despite the richness of the images we consume they will always describe somewhere else. These patterns are therefore unreliable. They are never true. While the patterns may be confusing because they describe somewhere else, for the very reason that they do describe the seductive "there", they are increasingly irresistible. Their unreliability might cause us to exercise some caution when we employ them, but in fact we appear to be compelled into seeking to interpret their meanings and apply their values to our design of "here". When we do transcribe these values into our design for "here" we are betrayed — our imagination is transfigured by the idealised version of a world whose limits we fail to see; the result is that we fashion someone else's fantasy.

Building 8 by Edmond & Corrigan inverts this problematic search for meaning in the metropolitan landscapes of the world and the scenic, frictionless trap they set. In designing Building 8 the architects have accepted the fact that any search for meaning within the post-industrial metropolis is going to produce paradoxical results. Instead, on the highly patterned surfaces of the building they have chosen to record messages of another type. These message sequences (or patterns) enable the building's occupants, and those passing the building in the street, to wander through a new type of information structure for the city and, in so doing, to personalise their experience.

Rather than mirror existing building decoration (or lack of it) Edmond & Corrigan has produced its own decorative scheme. Commentators who know the architects well might dismiss this approach as yet another of the architects' tributes to the theatre of suburban life. This sprawling world, which Australians have fashioned over the past 50 years, could be seen as one possible source among many for the patterns on Building 8, albeit not simply as a lexicon of colour and form. Such an evaluation categorises this work as a reflection of some suburban fantasy and thus their design as simply a romance.

Both architects are more capable authors than this. They did not attempt to create a fabric which can be read as a sum of recognisable signs. As stated, Building 8 is not proposed as a container of meaning. The building actually defies us to read it and make sense. Its dazzling and seductive surfaces cause us to suspend momentarily our dependence on the familiar patterns that historically have been described somewhere else. Instead of being seduced into this familiar role and our dependence on these patterns, as is our habit, we are enticed into contemplating Building 8 as it stands. At this point we are without the usual universal model as our support. It is then that the architects' intentions begin to unfold. While they intend that the building necessarily houses its occupants, they have also designed it to play a more important metropolitan role — that of a guide. This role is to guide us as we move — not through the city as a sum of beacons, but through a city now characterised less by its physical appearance than by its constantly changing information landscape (ie, the appearance of its appearance).

The stable pattern of human interaction with the city, based on our mobility through the metropolitan landscape, was the result of a simple choice between the actions — to depart, to arrive or to return. This pattern has been undermined by a new, metaphoric notion of movement. Instead of choosing to move, we are now mobilised in the pursuit of utopian images which our product-filled world projects. The daily rituals of living and working show no respect for directions. They are actions which are packaged in an elaborate vehicle travelling with increasing velocity through a landscape which refuses to yield any features that can be translated into recognisable universal meanings and values. The physical mobility which has characterised

and valorised most of the twentieth century is now almost insignificant in comparison to the mobility of information which is enticing us to tele-dwell as tele-characters who tele-communicate our tele-dreams. This causes us to re-define a more contingent methodology for observing and describing the world-as-found and projecting what-might-become.

Building 8 is such a projection. It is not about abstract form nor arbitrary ornamentation, it is about us, about our relationships with the world we have fashioned, about the information we exchange, about our relationships with each other. The abstraction and artifice of everyday life is the matter that Peter Corrigan has registered on Building 8. More than most he is aware that, as a result of the shift from the era of the production of "things" to the era of "self-production", our character is now imminent in our appearance. We no longer have any depth. Whereas it was always presumed that behind appearance there lay character, personality and more mysterious qualities, in the era of self-production this is no longer so. Therefore, before we explore the metropolitan landscape, we must construct that image of our "self" which we wish to project to others. But, like all journeys, in order to navigate this shifting landscape we need certain points of reference to find our way. In the information age the markers are no longer physical landmarks. The new markers now have become the sites containing the richest forms of information where our self-projections seem to best fit (see the growth of proposed new buildings with text naively applied to their exterior in an attempt to address this change as a literal exchange). However, the operation of this fit is heavily ironic. It works in two ways, as demonstrated in the following anecdote about one of the earliest commentators on our relationship to a changing information setting.

Tom Wolfe relates a story about taking Marshall McLuhan to dinner one evening with the intention of unhinging the always cool McLuhan. Wolfe took him without warning to a restaurant where the waitresses were topless. To his dismay McLuhan did not appear to be in the least phased by the incongruous nakedness, but looked intently at the setting for a moment without saying anything. Then he turned to Wolfe and stated: "These women are not naked". Wolfe then admits that he was a little phased at McLuhan's apparent blindness. He felt the need to point out that they were indeed naked. McLuhan paused, then again said emphatically: "These women are not naked — they are wearing us."

The passing restaurant gimmick of topless waitresses, which was staged to attract business, is an example of a setting being created where the appearance of appearance operates deceptively and into which our projections appear to fit. That conventional appearances and actuality might not equate should come as no surprise. It is the problem that confronts the city and our encounters with it.

The problem that confronts the city is not about continuing a design process which simply facilitates our ability to move across its surface. The problem is whether we, the pedestrians, given our pursuit of the sites of richest information, will continue to want to move through such a naked landscape as the city. Instead of adhering to the belief that we will always adapt our behaviour to the metropolitan landscape, the city must now develop ways of adapting itself to us. Instead of the banal display of the monuments to a misconstrued version of modernism that demands our submission, Building 8 marks a shift in the powerful relationship between the city and its citizens. In order to support us as we skim across this landscape the information structure of the metropolis has developed a strong surface tension. By contrast, the buildings in a city no longer appear to need a surface for any reason other than to protect their occupants from the elements.

Building 8 reverses the fate of modern buildings by possessing strongly patterned surfaces both inside and out, rich in information, which both mimic and support the myriad patterns we project in order to attract each other. It enters into the dialogue taking place on the street, reversing the roles between structure and behaviour. Whereas buildings have always been designed with the objective of providing a structure to which we adapt our behaviour, Building 8's structure has the capacity to adapt itself according to the message sequences we fashion daily for our navigation of the metropolitan landscape. It allows us to personalise the messages we exchange. It does not structure the information for us, but guides us toward a closer understanding of our complex relationship with the confusing world we are making and remaking constantly. While it may appear that Edmond and Corrigan have written on the building, in fact they have written on us.

Peter King

Renovatio:
Negative Dialectics for an (In)Visible College

"The Invisible College of the Rose Cross", Theophilus Schweighardt, 1618. From Yates, *The Rosicrucian Enlightenment*, Routlege & Kegan Paul, London, 1972, frontispiece and p.93.

On the right, the Hotel Der Fürstenhof has metamorphosed into the fat child of consumerism. Competition with the Hotel Palast has driven architecture to consume space and to wear a modish dress. It is more concerned with energy and presence than with significance. Its surfaces are not made to be read, but merely to entertain. They stimulate the consumption of architectural language until it loses all meaning or reference. They convey the transformation from a literate architecture to a physical architecture, a passage from mind to body. A first reading sees its swollen form as a direct product of the demand of hotel accommodations resulting from the railway. But what lies behind the mask? Out of what desire has it been formed? The great new roof gives a late-medieval cap to the walls, which form a strange blend of the classical and the mechanical. This is a deliberate fantasy that destroys the constraints of language and style, and destroys the narrow frames within which scholarship had limited the inheritance from past ages. It is a violation and a heresy, consuming the forms of past realities and giving freedom to our recollections of history. A second reading sees in the architectural forms an act of cultural subversion, an act that makes possible a compounding of realities, an act that destroys the autocratic power of architecture and mocks its mysteries.[1]

Another example of Vinteuil's key-phrases is that stonemason's geometry in the novels of Thomas Hardy.

[...] Do you remember the stonemasons in Jude the Obscure, and in The Well-Beloved the blocks of stone which the father hews out of the island coming in boats to be piled up in the son's workshop where they are turned into statues [...], and in short all those novels which can be superimposed on one another like the houses piled up vertically on the rocky soil of the island.[2]

The collage of the future will be executed without scissors or razor or glue etc, in short without any of the utensils that were necessary until now. It will leave behind the worktable and the artist's cardboard surfaces and it will take its place on the wall of the big city, the unlimited field of poetic achievements.[3]

1.THE WEST FACADE

Gazed at from the corner of Queen and A'Beckett
Streets, and framed by the buildings and foliage
that recede towards it along A'Beckett Street —
a frame that obtrudes and obscures, a supplement,
which, in Derrida's terms, both sites and besieges,
defines, and threatens to finish off by filling in
what it frames[4] the west facade of Building 8
seems to be all one wall, polychromatic mosaic-
work, with the exception of one fragment, an
unconformity, an uncorbelled oriel window[5]
(a memory of the College, and a memory of the
memory theatre of Robert Fludd, itself, as
Frances Yates has argued, a distortion of a
memory of Shakespeare's Globe Theatre for her
that distorted memory is an atemporal synthetic
idea of the entirety of that theatre, and as an idea
it is an "unlimited field of poetic achievements").[6]
As one moves down and up towards the
building along A'Beckett Street, as and in
"deliberate fantasy", the facade starts to
dimensionalise, to offer perspectives: at first,
it mounts, banks upward, as though it were an
analytical diagram of the receding and ascending
planes of a Poussin landscape (now in the Dorian
mode, now in the Phrygian),[7] the turret of the
single visible tower (studded with segmented
conoids) clenches into a fist (signing either
imprecation[8] or prestidigitation ["What am I
holding in this hand?"]); the tower itself bearing
up a sign of contradictory lightness, that which
should show the haecceities[9] of the wind, a
weather-vane, which is, however, here fixed
(in a "deliberate fantasy"), not signing wind but
will, the axes of the city's grid; the Scharoun-like
cloud/wave-forms of the vent, plant room —
and the artfully cantilevered, riotously yet
rigorously coloured, inspired as though it were
inflected by, and as though it were an index, of
the movement of the cloud/wave — flag-like
form of the Level 12 meeting room of the
Department of Architecture, parts of a "great
new roof", billow as signs of architectonic
cunning in imitatio, and as signs of an
architecture that cunningly exposes the

1 Alan Balfour, *Berlin: The Politics of Order:
1737-1989*, Rizzoli, New York, 1990,   pp.63-
64. Balfour is considering a 1932 photograph
(view toward the north) of Potsdamer Platz.
2 Marcel Proust, *The Captive* (*La prisonnière*,
1923), *Remembrance of Things Past* (*A la
recherche du temps perdu*, 1913-27, 1954),
trans. C. K. Scott-Moncrieff and Terence Martin;
and by Andreas Mayor, 3 vols, Penguin,
Harmondsworth, 1989 reprint), Vol III,
pp.382-83.
3 1936 statement by the second generation
surrealist Léo Malet, cited in Benjamin
H. D. Buchloh, "From Detail to Fragment:
Décollage Affichiste", October 56, Spring 1991,
p.99.
4 Jacques Derrida *On Grammatology* (*De la
grammatologie*, 1967), trans. Gayatri Spivak,
Johns Hopkins University Press, Baltimore, 1976.
5 "Unconformity" also has here a more personal
meaning: non-architectural (although the lack of
corbelling makes the oriel window not conform to
the standard definition of its type); but geological,
a petrography. The word reminds me of the rock
outcrop once present on Canberra's once extant
Capital Hill; both rocksite and hill were lost in the
construction of Giurgola's New Parliament House.
"An outcrop of rock at the summit of Capital Hill
displays an unconformity between the Black
Mountain Sandstone and the younger Silurian
Camp Hill Sandstone. This formation has been
described as a graphic and remarkable example of
an angular unconformity and is of educational and
scientific value. [...] While competitors may suggest
methods of preserving the unconformity on Capital
Hill, the Promoter accepts that preservation cannot
be assured". (Parliament House Construction
Authority, *Parliament House Canberra:
Conditions for a Two-stage Competition*, 2 vols,
Canberra, April 1979, Vol I, p.66.) The
competition entry by Norman Day Pty Ltd
(Project Designer: Howard Raggatt) retained the
outcrop. On this design, see Raggatt and Day,
statement in "Parliament House Competition: 9
Designs from Melbourne", *Transition*, 2,
November 1979, p.20.

6 Frances A. Yates, *Theatre of the World*,
Routledge & Kegan Paul, London and Henley,
1969. In this book Yates locates the design of the
Globe within the European Renaissance tradition of
bringing into contiguity and simultaneity ancient
cosmic meanings, religious meanings, profane
meanings, and magical meanings, all signified by
superimposed geometries, a "compounding" of
idealities; and suggests that although the
"long-vanished wooden building" (p.189) can never
be reconstructed the "idea" can abide and be
mobilised in its virtual occurrence, that is, its
non-occurrence. To adumbrate briefly an argument
discussed at some length below, form and idea are
evaporated from matter and condense into space,
subject matter, meaning. The atemporality I have
attributed to the apparition that is Yates' Globe is
perhaps valorised by the image of the atemporal
interrupting a mythical temporal that was (is)
apparently the sign of that theatre. Yates
(p.131, n.24) cites Edmond Malone: "But, though
the part appropriated to the audience was probably
circular, I now believe that the house was
denominated only from its sign; which was the
figure of Hercules supporting the Globe, under
which was written, *Totus mundus agit histrionem*".
(Malone, *Variorum* edition of Shakespeare's
Works, London, 1821, Vol III, p.67.) Hercules
only held up the world for a time that was an
interruption in and of the *temps durée*, to use
Bergson's phrase, of the classical mythological world-
picture; one of his Labours was to fetch the apples of
the Hesperides and Atlas offered to fetch them for
him if Hercules would carry the world while he was
doing it. Hercules agreed, and for a time out of time
the world was born by the one hero who had moved
most around and inside its spaces, the world
comprehended by its traveller (Hercules had to trick
Atlas back into place and bearing); this bit of
interrupted yet not arrested time, time without the
Bergsonian deterministic "intussusception", in
which the present is not added to the past but is
incorporated in it, and future time is only an
emanation, an aura, attracted to and playing over
this solid, comprehensive thing (and the time of the
Globe the type of which the interrupted time appears

to have been) was a cathected moment of "imaginary puissance", a sign of temps espace. (Shakespeare, Henry V, Chorus as prologue to Act One, l.25.)

[7] *"[...The classical theorists] called the Dorian mode steady, solemn and severe, and saw it as appropriate for serious, stern subjects full of wisdom. And, moving on from these by nature pleasant and joyful, they used the Phrygian when they wanted finer inflections and a higher pitch". (Nicolas Poussin, letter to Chantelou [Rome, 24 November 1647]. Cited and trans. in Alain Merot, Poussin, Hazan Editions, Paris, 1990, trans. Fabia Claris and Bridget Mason, Thames & Hudson, London, 1990, p.312.)*

[8] *Cf. the gesture performed by the stuffed, "moth-eaten and dusty" carcass of Don Fabrizio's once excitable Great Dane, Bendicò, dead for forty-five years, as it is finally thrown on the scrap-heap, "During the flight down from the window its form recomposed itself; in the air there seemed to be dancing a quadruped with long whiskers, its right leg raised in imprecation". (Giuseppe di Lampedusa, The Leopard [Il Gattopardo, 1958], trans. Archibald Colquhoun, The Reprint Society, London, 1961, p.223). Cf, also, "Only in the south, where a group of fists and fingers are thrust up through the soil, is the endless expanse interrupted. These fists and fingers are the Marabar Hills, containing the extraordinary caves". (E. M. Forster, A Passage To India [1924], Penguin, Harmondsworth, reprinted 1969, p.11.)*

[9] *"There is a mode of individuation very different from that of a person, subject, thing, or substance. We reserve the name haecceity for it. A season, a winter, a summer, an hour, a date, have a perfect individuality lacking nothing, even though this individuality is different from that of a thing or a subject. They are haecceities in the sense that they consist entirely of relations of movement and rest between molecules or particles, capacities to affect and be affected. When demonology expounds upon the diabolical art of local movements and transports of affect, it also notes the importance of rain, hail, wind, pestilential air, or air polluted by noxious particles, favourable conditions for these transports." (Gilles Deleuze and Félix Guattari, A Thousand Plateaus: Capitalism and Schizophrenia [Mille plateaux, 1980], trans. Brian Massumi, University of Minnesota Press, Minneapolis, third printing 1991, p.261.)*

[10] *This "organic" has little to do with that of Lloyd Wright: it is that biomorphism of the first person to apply this vexed and vexing epithet to architecture, Carlo Lodoli, as stated by Memmo, his biographer, and, even, that of, Hugo Häring: a "rational" architecture, "anatomically correct". (See Hanno-Walter Kruft, A History of Architectural Theory from Vitruvius to the Present (Geschichte der Architekturtheorie: Von der Antike bis zur Gegenwart, Verlag C. H. Beck, Munich, 1985, trans. Ronald Taylor, Elsie Callander, and Antony Wood, Zwemmer, London, and Princeton University Press, New York, 1994, p.197.)*

[11] *"In his Handbuch der literarischen Rhetorik [Manual of Literary Rhetoric], the standard reference in the field, Heinrich Lausberg, following the ancients, distinguishes the ordo naturalis from the ordo artificialis in composition. The first is that of the typical discourse and corresponds to an order given or desired by nature — or, as Lausberg adds with a touch of irony, to what habit makes us think as such. The ordo artificialis or artificiosus takes account of circumstances and the modifications they impose on the prescriptions of nature. That distinction, however, may be replaced or supplemented by another, which makes it possible to generalise principles that were conceived in terms of rhetoric. One would then distinguish an articulated composition from one that is not articulated (or does not appear to be). The model for this absence of a specific order would be, through a slight shift in the framework of the discourse, narration (especially oral narration) and description, both of which follow the natural order of events or perceptions without specific elaboration. As with the sentence, one would have to have given up on finding an order willed by nature or intended by spirit in the unfolding of the discourse." (Pierre Missac, Walter Benjamin's*

unfaithfulness to, and willed loss of, the momenta of the organic.[10]   When the organic is beefed up, or beetled down, in material and scale into architecture it, almost irredeemably, loses its virtù and pulse, yet architecture still may cancel its own unavoidable loss of life, but only if it affirms, in its own rhetoric,[11] that life is auratic or indwelling, resounds over, or redounds in, architectural form, or even only subsists (or is alluded to, or abides) in it; even in the seemingly perversely vigorous expressiveness of such an intellectual and physical construct as Loosian architecture: architecture that achieves its telos in death, as Denkmal or Grabmal ("memorial" or "tomb"). What abides (the virtù and pulse of that "life"; its after-images, after-feelings, after-sounds) in design, is as an apparition; it appears to live as an insistent desire, seemingly and optatively, to shimmer or blast out, perhaps as an appeal to — a Mahlerian trumpeting, an Appel, in his Fourth Symphony on stage, interior to it, in his Second Symphony, behind it, more interior, inniger, yet also, out there, somewhere from which the noises of that space are drawn into, and inflect, it — or attractor, or, even, as an abiding enactment of, ethics (the ideational figure architecture still abides, even though its spaces might be disfigured or lost), and fragments (evidence of loss and retrospective hope of rebuilding or of building a new res)[12], of an ethical spatiality,[13] perhaps of the College or the Globe. The cloud/wave forms of Building 8's roof seem to fling the segmented Level 12 cornice along like rain or sand beneath them; and then, as one moves closer from Elizabeth Street, the power of that which had been invisible at Queen Street comes into play; the setbacks — the width of which remains hidden — implode, or, better, impulse, the building so that it seems to compress into a great force, contracting into an apprehensible but latent formal and mass-effect abundance.[14] When Building 8 is viewed from the junction of, and aperture offered by (and designed for), A'Beckett and Swanston Streets: the upper levels of the building are masked by the raked cornice of the Level 8 terrace; the downpipes — and perhaps this apparition is in part mediated by the rake of the cornice — seem to shine forth as epigones or, even, retrograde yet renovated futurist epitomes, of part of Sullivan's Swedenborgian *"grammar of ornament based on organic (embryonic) and inorganic (geometric) basic forms, in which through the overlapping of divisions and expansions, human power shows itself in action,"*[15] or of a now made apprehensible vicissitude of that "grammar," (the conic section could be a metal inorganic abstraction of the thighs and pudenda of the talismanic Venus of Willendorf); so much of the visible protuberant fenestration seems to be fantasies after Wilhelm Wundt's visually ambiguous now raised and now recessed pyramids, which demonstrate the ambivalence or duality of vision (perhaps these were found while flicking through a book on Malevich in the office's library);[16] the great black truss recalls the metal-work of Viollet-le-Duc;[17] beneath this is a fountain, with a low-lying, flattened pyramid as its finial,[18] set in a triangle, pouring out clear water in a regular unenthralling cascade from broad, neither wide nor generous slits (perhaps a critical comment on the rapid unspectacular regulated throughput of students and staff enforced upon, and taken up by, universities by the Dawkins plan and the subsequent quality audits annually imposed by the Labor Government; the proximity of this joyless slitted thing to the ATM of the Commonwealth Bank on Level 1 is possibly a jibe also); above the ground-level fire escape doors are mean sections through the characteristic pendant step-like gradient of Portoghesi (what Portoghesi calls "echo effects,"[19] but where is the mirrored and mirroring, gazing Narcissus for whom Echo pines and fades?); beside these are palm trees[20] manacled to the building by small-scale Viollet-le-Duc protheses; set back behind truss, fountain, fire escapes, and trees, the pre-existing Union Building of John Andrews (1977-83) over which Building 8 looms, and on which it squats, has become nothing more than a bas-de-page,[21] laconically doodled upon, inflected with

a few coloured glass panes to tie it in with the large glass wall of the south-east facade; the scale of the assemblage that is the now visible facade never really seems to settle — the whole facade, in its horizontal expanse and with its vertical setbacks, is never completely visible — a blinkered eye would see it as domestic in scale, its polychromatic panels no larger than those of the Charman House (1983-84), yet when it is viewed next to the English Palladian Storey Hall it is huge, and, due to the Level 8 cornice, a lot of that hugeness is hidden, a mounting presence held in, and either perturbing or exciting, the memory; moreover, as so much of the above account has suggested, the facade is riddled with, and riddles by, allusions and fragments.

It is not so much a written grammar, as woven grammata.[22] Its inlaid stories are overcoded stories — like those of the Wessex of the poet, novelist, and architect Thomas Hardy, which overcoded Dorset, Somerset, Devon, and Cornwall into a "looking glass", a fictive, yet sometimes factive, temporal, yet sometimes atemporal, geographically true, yet sometimes distorted, uncanny, "progressive and uncertain" realm,[23] in which many locations are foci, keepers or prompters of stories that fragment the real historical, administrative, social, agricultural, architectural and geographical conditions into "the stonemason's geometry" Proust's narrator speaks of; Wessex and the real territorial divisions (all are composed productions, as is the west facade) are in a metonymic relation, yet there is hysteresis where they touch, and this hysteresis is a cathecting that fills the fragments of Hardy's game. And fills, in a similar fashion, the game of the west facade and its presence (or presences) in the city. As Massimo Cacciari writes (although his subject is the Loosian house):

That which can be shown is not the "redemption" of place, but the dissonance existing between the

Passages [Passage de Walter Benjamin, 1987], trans. Shierry Weber Nicholsen, The MIT Press, Cambridge, Mass. and London, 1995, p.126. He cites Lausberg, Handbuch der literarischen Rhetorik, Hueber, Munich, 1973, p.245.)

12   On res as "conceptual content", see citation and n.32, below.

13   See E. H. Gombrich, "The Subject of Poussin's Orion" (1944), in Symbolic Images: Studies in the Art of the Renaissance II, Phaidon, Oxford, second edition in small format, 1978, pp.119-22.

14   On "mass-effect" and its "pregnant quality" as a peculiarly "purely visual art", see Adrian Stokes, The Quattro Cento (1932), in The Critical Writings of Adrian Stokes, ed. Lawrence Gowing, 3 vols, Thames & Hudson, London, 1978, Vol I, pp.134-37. On "contracting-into-abundance", see Michael Tippett, Moving Into Aquarius, Paladin, London, 1974, pp.19-27.

15   Kruft, op cit, p.359.

16   Illustrated and discussed in Larissa A. Zhadova, Malevich: Suprematism and Revolution in Russian Art 1910 - 1930 (1978), trans. Alexander Lieven Thames & Hudson, London, 1982, p.46.

17   "Eugène-Emmanuel Viollet-le-Duc, 'Entretiens sur l'Architecture, Vol. II, 1872. Vaulted hall of metal and brick construction'". (Caption and illustration in Kruft, op cit, pl.156.)

18   This pyramid is certainly not of the kind described by G. R. Levy: "At this period [of the early dynasties], by the gigantic efforts of engineers, builders and craftsmen, the Pyramid towered always nearer to the sky, but only the Gods might mount its sloping sides". (Levy, The Gate of Horn: A Study of the Religious Conceptions of the Stone Age and Their Influence upon European Thought, Faber & Faber, London, 1963, p.173.) It, however, might signify the futility of pyramid selling.

19   Cited in Rudolf Arnheim, The Dynamics of Architectural Form, University of

California Press, Berkeley, Los Angeles, London, 1977, p.237.

[20] Merely exotica? Signifiers of imperialism and/or victory? Or symbols of the "palm, which bears its profusion between earth and heaven", the symbol assigned to Benjamin's writings by Pierre Missac? (Missac, op cit, p.39.)

[21] On the bas-de-page, see Christopher S. Wood, Albrecht Altdorfer and the Origins of German Landscape, Reaktion Books, London, 1993, p.37.

[22] Ann L. T. Bergren has pointed out that the Ancient Greek "grammata" can mean either "pictures" or "writing". See her "Language and the Female in Early Greek Thought", Arethusa, 16, No 1/2, Spring/Fall 1983, pp.71-73. Cf, also, Walter Benjamin: "CAUTION: STEPS

Work on good prose has three steps: a musical stage when it is composed, an architectonic one when it is built, and a textile one when it is woven". (Walter Benjamin, One-Way Street [Einbahnstraße, 1928], in One-Way Street and Other Writings, trans. Edmund Jephcott and Kingsley Shorter, Verso, London, reprinted 1992, p.61.)

[23] Thomas Hardy, "Preface" (1895) to A Pair Of Blue Eyes (1873, 1912), in The New Wessex Edition, gen. ed. P. N. Furbank, Macmillan, London, hardback edition 1976, p.31. All references to Hardy's novels will be to this edition.

[24] Massimo Cacciari, Architecture and Nihilism: On the Philosophy of Modern Architecture, trans. Stephen Sartarelli, Yale University Press, New Haven and London, 1993, p.172.

[25] Cf in A Pair of Blue Eyes, Knight's sudden epiphany, or non-sublime sensing of the concatenated aporias and pressures of the abyssal, a spatio-temporal conflation, his seeing of the abiding fossilised Trilobite embedded in the "Cliff without a Name", just as he has fallen and is imperilled; he clings to the face of the cliff, flattened, hanging there, facing into it, and "engaging" in "metaphors" of permanence and geological contiguity — these metaphors are forced into metonyms by the actions of "a most powerful

mechanism" — as Elfriede (invisible to him) tears up her undergarments to construct a rope by which he can be pulled up. The conjunction of the dangerous predicament, the vision of the prehistoric past, and the invisible eroticised stripping present is an attractor for Hardy's prose (and verse), particularly, as here, in a place of auratic emanation or phantasmagoria, a place such as the "Cliff without a Name", where "the bloom [as of 'a Hambro' grape] seemed to float off into the atmosphere, and inspire terror through the lungs". (Hardy, A Pair of Blue Eyes, pp.218, 222.) On "metaphors" in extremis and the "most powerful mechanism", see A. David Napier, Foreign Bodies: Performance, Art, and Symbolic Anthropology, University of California Press, Berkeley and Los Angeles, 1992, pp.198-99.

[26] Hardy, Jude the Obscure (1896, 1912), p.46.

[27] Hardy, The Well-Beloved (1897, 1912), p.28.

[28] "Never shall I be able to say, what this place is like, dear friend (that would be language such as the angels use among men), but the very fact that it is, that it exists, you must believe me blindly. It couldn't be described to anybody, it is utterly right, yes, in a flash I understood the legend that God, when he took the sun on the fourth day and placed it, set it exactly above Toledo: so sidereal is the situation of this prodigious city, so outward, so much in space [...]." (Rainer Maria Rilke, letter to the Princess Marie von Thurn und Taxis-Hohenlohe, All Souls' Day, 1912, in Rilke, Selected Letters 1902-1926, trans. R. F. C. Hull, Quartet Books, London, 1988, p.219.)

[29] Maurice Blanchot, The Writing of the Disaster (L'Écriture du désastre, 1980), trans. Ann Smock, University of Nebraska Press, Lincoln and London, third paperback printing 1992, p.60.

[30] Kruft, op cit, p.442.

[31] T. S. Eliot, "The Waste Land" (1922), in The Complete Poems and Plays of T. S. Eliot, Faber & Faber, London, 1969, p.75, l.430.

[32] Wood, op cit, p.49.

[33] Mies van der Rohe, "Where Do We Go From Here?", Bauen und Wohnen, 15, No. 11, 1960, p.391. Cited in Fritz Neumeyer, The Artless Word: Mies van der Rohe on the Building Art (Mies van der Rohe. Das kunstlose Wort. Gedanken zur Baukunst, 1986), trans. Mark Jarzombek, The MIT Press, Cambridge, Mass. and London, 1991, p.332.

equivalence of technico-scientific space and the characteristic of space as a game of a combination of places where things are gathered and dwell with man. This dissonance must be composed: even the extreme dissonances must be the object of composition.[24]

The city composition of the walk from Queen Street to Swanston Street, as one keeps intent on the facade, is a movement (a double movement between desired vision and its supplement: a risked, bulking, occlusion, [miraging, as that which simultaneously blinds and transfigures the contiguity, pentratration, flaying, withdrawing, distance — and those loci particular to Hardy — forcible in affect, in an amalgam of distance or spatio-temporal proximity or/and, sundering, tearing the two apart])[25] from the boy Jude's enraptured vision of Christminster (Oxford) to the young man Pierston's re-experiencing of the "Gibraltar of Wessex" (Portland), and is also a compounding, the combination and dissonance of the two places:

Some way within the limits of the stretch of landscape, points of light like the topaz gleamed. The air increased in transparency with the lapse of minutes, till the topaz points showed themselves to be the vanes, windows, wet roof slates, and other shining spots upon the spires, domes, freestone-work, and varied outlines that were faintly revealed. It was Christminster, unquestionably; either directly seen, or miraged in the peculiar atmosphere.[26]

More than ever the spot seemed what it was said once to have been, the ancient Vindilia Island, and the Home of the Slingers. The towering rock, the houses above houses, one man's doorstep rising behind his neighbour's chimney, the gardens hung up by one edge to the sky, the vegetables growing on apparently almost vertical planes, the unity of the whole island as a solid and single block of limestone four miles long, were no longer familiar and commonplace ideas. All now stood dazzlingly unique and white against the tinted sea, and the sun flashed on infinitely stratified walls of oolite,
The melancholy ruins
Of cancelled cycles,...
with a distinctiveness that called the eyes to it as strongly as any spectacle he had beheld afar.[27]

What Hardy achieves in these passages is the fragmenting of the two places — one as a fleeting, yet forever-desired, abiding vision, and the other as a petrographic, abiding set of oddities set in a bedazzled coherent space that itself is a fragment, constructed out of fragments, an unconformity — out of the real physical location, and out of the presently operating supplementary silence of all the rest of Wessex (all that which is not being written about, a mounting absence held in, and either perturbing or exciting, the memory). In Hardy's novels Wessex is a sidereal space in which various constellations intermittently but unforgettably emerge from the clouds that so frequently obscure the stars, the supplement to the clouds, the supplement to Wessex; when they emerge their site is as star-like, as charged, as Rilke's Toledo.[28] This achievement is analogous to that of Edmond & Corrigan in the facade. Maurice Blanchot writes:

Fragmentation, the mark of a coherence all the firmer in that it has to come undone in order to be reached, and reached not through a dispersed system, or through dispersion as a system, for fragmentation is the pulling to pieces (the tearing) of that which never has pre-existed (really or ideally as a whole, nor can it be reassembled in any future presence whatever. Fragmentation is the spacing, the separation effected by a temporalisation which can only be understood — fallaciously — as the absence of time.[29]

The design of the facade effects that "spacing" in its composition of fragments that have never been torn into a space in this way before. The façade is not an accretion like Horace Walpole's Strawberry Hill (1750-94), or a museum of fragments from the fabled Abendland (Europe) as inset in the ground floor exterior wall of Cass Gilbert's Woolworth Building (1911-13), and it is certainly not "the picture-postcard world [...,] a piece of three-dimensional Pop Art masquerading as architecture" that is Charles Moore's New Orleans Piazza d'Italia (1977-78);[30] but a hermeneutic constellation of fragments and spaces as form and formative,

resumption not "consumption", as architecture parlante it speaks to the city: "These fragments I have shored against my ruins."[31] Torn from their points on the here/there/where? and past/present/when? space-time (dis)continuum, they become matter in the moment of translation into subject-matter. This translation has been clearly stated by Christopher S. Wood:

Subject-matter is something subjected to a telling. Subject-matter is thus more or less equivalent to Aristotle's logos or argument, the primary imitation of action that serves as the raw material for plot or mythos. Classical rhetorical theory acknowledged an equivalent hierarchy between materia, or raw material, and res, or conceptual content. Medieval and Renaissance epic drew its plots from an unformed stock of characters and events it called "matter", for example, the "matter of Britain" (the Arthurian legends or the "matter of Troy".[32]

This statement sheds light on both Hardy's translation of the places and plots of the real counties into the "matter of Wessex" and Edmond & Corrigan's engagement with the "matter of architecture". Wood's declaration of equivalence recalls the incantatory maxim Mies van der Rohe (shoring up his own ruins) tore from Aquinas: "adaequatio intellectus et rei" ("congruence of thought and thing", or as Wood has it, "conceptual content").[33] As a self-styled "modern philosopher", Mies goes on to gloss this as "truth means facts".[34] Mies, getting at the truth of the matter, goes on to glass, and, according to Cacciari, *"[t]ransparence in Mies is absolute because it is born out of the precise and truly desperate awareness that there is nothing left to 'collect' and hence, to make transparent".* [35] Mies preserves "the symbol in the invisible".[36] In Cacciari's interpretation, the symbol here "is the place where the city once 'dwelled'; once this place is used up, the struggle against devouring time, which is the purpose of the lawmaker-architect, is inexorably consigned to the process of becoming".[37] Mies performs the revelatory (knowledge acquired through an intensifying sequence of interrogations) and consequent self- and world-punitive (blinding, the world made invisible) deeds of the Oedipus myths.

[34] Ibid., loc cit.

[35] Cacciari, op cit, p.190.

[36] Ibid., p.206.

[37] Ibid., loc cit.

[38] On solicitation, see Alan Bass's "Translator's Introduction" to Jacques Derrida, Writing and Difference (L'écriture et la différence, 1967), trans. Bass, University of Chicago Press, Chicago, 1978, p.xvi. "[S]olicitation [...] derives from the Latin sollicitare, meaning to shake the totality, from sollus, "all", and ciere, "to move, to shake" [...]."

[39] Rilke, Briefe aus Muzot, pp.334-38. Cited and trans. in Duino Elegies (Duino Elegien, 1922), the German text trans. with introduction and commentary by J. B. Leishman and Stephen Spender, Chatto & Windus, London, paperback edition 1975, pp.157-59.

[40] Rilke, Duino Elegies, ed cit, pp.86-87. Translation modified.

[41] Ibid., loc cit.

[42] "[T]he category of indicial signs of a noniconic character endowed with both syntactic and semantic marks. The syntactic marks are longitude, apicality, movement, dynamic force; the semantic marks are direction, proximity, distance." (Claude Gandelman, Reading Pictures, Viewing Texts, Indiana University Press, Bloomington and Indianapolis, 1991, p.28.)

[43] Gershom Scholem, Major Trends in Jewish Mysticism (1941, revised 1946), Schocken Books, New York, first paperback edition 1961, pp.26-27. Scholem cites Friedrich Creuzer, Symbolik und Mythologie der alten Völker (1810), Vol. I, p.70.

[44] Cf, however, Gombrich's reading of Creuzer: "Creuzer insisted explicitly on the distinction between this notion of the symbol and that of a mere emblem which he feels to be entirely devoid of that significant dignity. What marks the symbol is precisely its

The symbol is secure in the invisible because its operation is in a twofold suspension, in extinction (an Entortung, liquidation of space), and in becoming (a solicitation[38] of time, in which all events are evaporated into eventualities). This invisible is that which out of, in the Duino Elegies, Rilke's blinded angel, by gazing inward, is able to escape and, for a torn yet cathected, enchanted yet despairing moment, in the otherwise reifying and celebratory Ninth Elegy, into which the earth, "the dear visible and tangible", desires to disappear and become "the vibration and agitation of our own nature".[39]

Erde, ist es nicht dies, was du willst: u n s i c h t b a r
in uns erstehn? — Ist es dein Traum nicht,
einmal unsichtbar zu sein? — Erde! unsichtbar!
Was, wenn Verwandlung nicht, ist dein drängender
Auftrag?
(Earth is it not this you want: to arise
invisibly in us? Is it not your dream
to be invisible one day? Earth! Invisible!
What, if not transformation, is your insistent command?)[40]

As Rilke insists, Edmond & Corrigan "show" and "tell" the Angel "things"[41] in "vibration and agitation": not in the invisible yet palpable, but in a palpable apparition. They exhibit the symbol in the apprehensible and comprehensive slippage between thing (Ding) and comprehended notion or concept (Begriff). But the slippage is not a veering off into the metaphysical: the Verwandlung itself remains a thing gesturing toward the idea — it simulates the res in its dissimulation of materia. By employing ostention,[42] they locate the symbolic in the fates and phantasmagoria of matter. The practice (dragging its clients with it) plods in Heideggerian Holzwege (paths through, and labyrinths within, the forest) after brief sightings of a quarry, perhaps Gershom Scholem's (following Creuzer) sudden incandescent illumination of the symbol.

In the mystical symbol a reality which in itself has, for us, no form or shape becomes transparent and, as it were, visible, through the medium of another reality which clothes its content with visible and expressible meaning, as for example the cross for the Christian. The thing which becomes a symbol retains its original form and its original content. It does not become, so to speak, an empty shell into which another content is poured; in itself, through its own existence, it makes another reality transparent which cannot appear in any other form. If allegory can be defined as the representation of an expressible something by another expressible something, the mystical symbol is an expressible representation of something which lies beyond the sphere of expression and communication, something which comes from a sphere whose face is, as it were, turned inward and away from us. A hidden and inexpressible reality finds its expression in the symbol. If the symbol is thus also a sign or representation it is nevertheless more than that.

For the Kabbalist, too, every existing thing is endlessly correlated with the whole of creation; for him, too, everything mirrors everything else. But beyond that he discovers something else which is not covered by the allegorical network: a reflection of the true transcendence. The symbol signifies nothing and communicates nothing, but makes something transparent which is beyond all expression. Where deeper insight into the structure of the allegory uncovers fresh layers of meaning, the symbol is intuitively understood all at once — or not at all. The symbol in which the life of the Creator and that of creation become one, is — to use Creuzer's words — "a beam of light which, from the dark and abysmal depths of existence and cognition, falls into our eye and penetrates our whole being". It is a "momentary totality" which is perceived in a mystical now — the dimension of time proper to the symbol.[43]

In this effusion the invisible is lost, or made visible, in the transparent:[44] the manners of matter are the seemings of yet more matter that seems to matter. Edmond & Corrigan, as artificers, as Cretans (and all Cretans are liars), get at the seemings, the untruth of matter — cf. the oxymoron that nowadays is the title of Derrida's The Truth in

Painting, as a phrase, this title was once an urgent telos for Ruskin — and the true miming of matter's manners in unveiling and producing form and idea.

Since the mime imitates nothing, represents nothing, opens up in its origin the very thing he is tracing out, he must be the very movement of truth. Not, of course, truth in the form of adequacy between the representation and the present of the thing itself, or between the imitator and the imitated, but truth as the present unveiling of the present, monstration, manifestation, production, aletheia.[45]

The etymology of aletheia has always been a vexed thing: for Plato in the Cratylus it meant "divine wandering", Heidegger "by a verbal analysis" interpreted it as Unverborgenheit, "a state of lacking shelter and protection", exposure, and this state returns us to a "wandering" that is no longer "divine".[46] Yet the two meanings co-exist in a non-identicality. As do the simultaneous nothingness and manifestation of the mime; and the simultaneous fragmentation and composition, an adaequatio materiae et rei, of the facade. The non-identicality of the facade is non-unified, temporal in its "thin slice, held between the contiguous impressions that composed our life at that time; the memory of a particular image is but regret for a particular moment, and houses, roads, avenues are as fugitive, alas, as the years",[47] yet, as idea and form, it is a renovatio,[48] an atemporal (not only does it mark time but it is marked by time, altered, extended, in what it has torn out of it) and perhaps provocatively untimely, contiguous (in where it has torn things to, more alteration and extension) entirety. As part of Building 8, which won the office an Award of Merit in the Institutional Alterations and Extensions section from the Victorian chapter of the RAIA, the west façade enacts the "happy revolution" adumbrated in, as "a strange blend of the classical and the mechanical", Viollet-le-Duc's Dictionnaire: "To restore a building is not to repair or rebuild it but to re-establish it in a state of entirety which might never have existed at any given moment".[49]

2. EXTERIORS

Robert Klein has commented on other projects that are entireties yet are not comprehended as single identities:

The subtlety and complexity of schemes invented by scholars and beaux esprits of the Mannerist period for the decoration of palaces and residences — even for the triumphal entries of sovereigns were so great that no spectator of average intelligence and culture could hope to understand them in the time he would normally spend looking at them. Concerning the designs for a festive entry celebrating the wedding of Ferdinand de Medici in 1589, Aby Warburg remarks that even the authors of the printed descriptions seemed unaware of the meaning of the Trionfo invented by Bardi.[50]

In an essay "Modern Painting and Phenomenology", Klein appears to return to the concerns of indecipherable communality in performance and architecture expressed above; for himself, as art historian, his job condemns him to "the slow agony of reference"[51] in an ever-expanding library.[52] Robin Evans, writing on fragmentation, has cautioned:

As soon as we identify something as broken, we become detectives of its history. What larger entity was it detached from? How did it end up in bits — or, with our modified definition [a fragment is something that looks as if it has been broken], how are we to imagine it got that way?[53]

Merleau-Ponty identified a prejudice in the practice of visual reference in which the object under scrutiny possesses an a priori individuated language — almost a Derrida-like "arche-writing". When this speech which precedes speech (Ursprache or Idspeak), is uttered it unleashes a sociogenesis that appears to be primal, a "fulfilment" of a infantile lack or loss, cultured, the speech achieving "a certain point of perfection", and political, economical, and even sports-crazy, a celebration of an "achievement".

clouding darkness, which is of course incompatible with the clarity of a sign." (Gombrich, "Icones Symbolicae: Philosophies of Symbolism and their Bearing on Art", in op cit, p.188.) Is the symbol dazzle or shadow?

[45] *Derrida, Dissemination, trans. Barbara Johnson, University of Chicago Press, Chicago, 1981, pp.205-06. Cited in Yve-Alain Bois, Painting as Model, The MIT Press, Cambridge, Mass. and London, pp.154-55.*

[46] *Blanchot, op cit pp.94-95. Filarete, in his Trattato di architettura (1461-65?), publishes an image of Adam exposed to the elements, sheltering himself with raised arms. (Illustration in Kruft, op cit, pl.7.)*

[47] *Proust, Swann's Way (Du côté de chez Swann, 1913), op cit, Vol.I, p.462.*

[48] *On renovatio as desired but deferred "renewal or rebirth or rediscovery of the past through which a new future is created", see Yates, Astraea: The Imperial Theme in the Sixteenth Century (1975), Pimlico, London, 1993, passim.*

[49] *Viollet-le-Duc, Dictionnaire raisonné de l'architecture française du XI⁻ au XVI⁻ siècle (10 vols., Paris, 1854-68), Vol.VIII, p.14. (Cited in Kruft, op cit, p.284.)*

[50] *Robert Klein, Form and Meaning (La forme et l'intelligible, 1970), trans. Madeleine Jay and Leon Wieseltier with a foreword by Henri Zerner, The Viking Press, New York, 1979, p.43. Some essays in the French original have not been included in the translated edition. Klein cites Warburg, "I costumi teatrali per gli intermezzi del 1589", in Gesammelte Schriften (Leipzig-Berlin) Vol.I, pp.280-82.*

[51] *Klein, op cit, p.185.*

[52] *This, if he is passionate, and Klein was, forces him into the Trauerarbeit ("work of mourning") undergone by Proust's narrator. "A great weakness no doubt for a person, to consist merely of a collection of moments; a great strength also: he is a product of memory,*

and our memory of a moment is not informed of everything that has happened since; this moment which it has recorded endures still, lives still, and with it the person whose form is outlined in it. And, moreover, this disintegration does not only make the dead one live, it multiplies him or her. In order to be consoled I would have to forget, not one, but innumerable Albertines. When I had succeeded in bearing the grief of losing this Albertine, I must begin again with another, with a hundred others." (Proust, *The Fugitive* [*Albertine disparue*, 1925], op cit, Vol.III, p.487.) The forgetting is a making of iconography and history.

53 Robin Evans, *The Projective Cast: Architecture and its Three Geometries*, The MIT Press, Cambridge, Mass. and London, 1995, p.56.

54 "[L]ife aspires to absolute totality [...] to the science of sciences — philosophy [...] aspires to architecture, which is a threefold totality: it contains all the other arts within itself — painting, sculpture, the art of building, the art of gardens [...] It is the place of the totality of human life on earth." (P. Bommersheim, "Philosophy and Architecture", published in 1920 in *Frühlicht*. Cited and trans in Cacciari, op cit, p.127.)

55 Maurice Merleau-Ponty, "Le Langage indirect et les voix du silence", in *Les Temps modernes*, June 1952, p.2123. Cited and trans. in Klein, op cit, p.185.

56 Klein, op cit, p.184.

57 Wood, op cit, p.29.

58 Rilke, *Duino Elegies*, ed cit, p.24.

59 Illustration in Manfredo Tafuri, *The Sphere and the Labyrinth: Avant-Gardes and Architecture from Piranesi to the 1970s* (*La sfera e il labirinto: Avanguardie e architettura da Piranesi agli anni '70*, 1980), trans. Pellegrino d'Acierno and Robert Connolly, The MIT Press, Cambridge, Mass., 1987, pl.6. "As in the *Carceri*, what at first seems to be the subject is later negated and turned into a supplementary element. The centrality of the composition, with its successive and independent rings, projects outward from the circular space of the grand staircase subdivided into eight flights,

which, among the organisms 'that are in search of their own role' within the concentric structures, is, significantly , one of the minor spaces. Actually, as one proceeds gradually from the centre toward the periphery of the composition, the dimension of the rooms seems to grow progressively larger, while their geometrical structure becomes increasingly more differentiated and articulated. For example, look at the succession of loggias and atriums on the perpendicular axes or, even more revealing, the succession of spaces juxtaposed on the diagonal axes, terminating — at the bottom half of the sheet — in two mixtilinear rooms with a boldly carved out perimeter. What differentiates Piranesi's design from the abstract designs 'of great dimension', so customary in the eighteenth-century competitions of the Academy of San Luca, is its obvious programmatic character. The 'ampio magnifico Collegio' is in fact a structure theoretically endlessly expandable. The independence of the parts and their montage obey no other law than that of pure contiguity. The Collegio, then, constitutes a kind of gigantic question mark on the meaning of architectural composition: the 'clarity' of the planimetric choice is subtly eroded by the process with which the various parts engage in mutual dialogue; the single space secretly undermines the laws to which it pretends to subject itself". (Ibid., op cit, pp.30-31.) For an excellent account of Tafuri's *machine infernale*, see Margaret Plant, "The Nostalgia of Manfredo Tafuri", in *Transition*, Nos. 27/28, Summer/Autumn 1989, pp.105-11.

60 Jean Paulhan, *L'Art informel* (Paris, 1962), p.45. Cited and trans. in Klein, op cit, p.190.

61 Cacciari, op cit, p.166.

62 "Intensity cannot be called high or low without reestablishing the scale of values and principles characteristic of moderation's mediocre reality. Be it exertion or inertia, intensity is the extreme of difference, in excess of the being that ontology takes for granted. Intensity is an excess, an absolute disruption which admits of no regimen, region, regulation, direction, erection, insur-rection, nor does it admit of their simple contraries; thus it

This is a Nuremberg rally, synaesthetic, anaesthetic, pan-aesthetic,[54] a social oncology, "which will compel the assent of all".[55] Although Merleau-Ponty is here critical of the "prejudice", he is in fact describing the mechanisms of the phenomenological project, which Klein states to be "a contamination of the language of criticism", in its desire to reduce the manifold to the unfolded and disentangled, a universale Selbstbestimmung (a determined "universal self-determination").[56]

So Klein's dilemma remains: how to speak of a sociogenic project or object (e.g., Building 8) that aspires to transform and mobilise, make perform, its physical context, res, and materia, (the decoration of palaces and the entries of sovereigns were temporary spaces that figured forth, or incandesced, a transfigured image or imago sublating historia,[57] yet apparently, were only for a few, a gedeutete Welt ["interpreted world"],[58] and were, finally, an image of an absolutist state) without putting it into jackboots or making it dance en masse at Mathildenhöhe or losing oneself in a Piranesian prison of texts, an ampio magnifico Collegio of arcings, loops and stairs?[59] Jean Paulhan, whom Klein sets up against Merleau-Ponty in a diabolical dialectics, merely rehearses in, of all places, "limbo", the equivalence of intellect and thing that Mies performs: for Paulhan, "limbo" is "where thought is not distinct from things".[60] There are many clews through Klein's maze in performances, films, texts, projects, and objects. The recent writings, however, of the Lacanian Joan Copjec, when wilfully misread, on sociogenesis, and when experienced and contemplated, the aspiring generous space-making (Freigabe von Orten)[61] facades and some of the public spaces of Building 8, and of its unacknowledged and probably unknown type and maquette, the Stuttgart Liederhalle (although in 1949 Scharoun's design was premiated, the assemblage of delicately differentiated and unconforming façades was built to the designs of Rolf Gutbrod and Adolf Abel in the 1950s) possibly assuage (or, perversely, in their flayed and flaying intensity,[62] increase) the agony. Copjec writes:

The construction of the subject depends [...] on the subject's taking social representations as images of its own ideal being, on the subject's deriving a "narcissistic pleasure" from these representations. This notion of pleasure, however vaguely evoked, is what makes the argument for construction stick; it "cements" or "glues" the realm of the psychic to that of the social. (Hume described cause as the "cement of the universe" — the metaphor helps to determine a certain conception of cause.) The point of insertion of the subject into society thus becomes a point of resemblance, convergence, attachment.[63]

Copjec herself gags at this, and raises two images (one from Freud on mensuration — a "denatured" and supposedly denaturing "inch" — imposed on the size of a "suckling", and the other from Beckett's novel Watt in which a committee of five men is unable to look at each other in the minimum necessary twenty looks, "every man looking four times") to counter the indwelling complexities in it, complexities that are currently "razed" and proposes the "sacrifice" of some ill-defined "brain-mind"[64] bit — a part of which seems to be the look that misses (who knows, it might a human mimicry of the ingazing of Rilke's angel?) — as the entrée into society;[65] she writes for and in the "limbo" Paulhan had mucked about in; both write of the "denaturing" of the subject, of its alienation,[66] and both seemingly unwittingly — she in naming, he in self-absorption — valorise the non-identity and entirety of Narcissus and his transmutation from matter into the manners of space and discourse. As Blanchot writes:

[W]e ought to rather consider that Narcissus, seeing the image he does not recognise,[67] sees in it the divine aspect, the nonliving, eternal part (for the image is incorruptible) which, without his knowing it, is his and which he does not have the right to look at, lest he fall prey to a vain desire. Thus one might say that he dies (if he dies) of being immortal, of having the immortality of appearance — the immortality which his metamorphosis into a flower attests: a funereal flower or flower of rhetoric.[68]

Narcissus had lived under an interdiction: that he never was to see himself. He was all environment. When he breaks the ban and looks, he does not

necessarily fulfil the command "know thyself!" (or go through the Lacanian fiction of "the Mirror Stage"), but he becomes a locus and acquires a telos and speech, a soliloquy indited by Ovid: "Possession dispossessed me",[69] an anticipation, a pre-echo, of Freud's dictum, in his New Introductory Lectures on Psychoanalysis (1932), of "Where it [id] was, there should I [ego] come to be" and Freud's comment on this reclamation and renovatio: "It is a cultural achievement somewhat like the draining of the Zuyder Zee".[70] We now have to "denature" horticulture parlante into the architecture parlante of Building 8.

We start to do this by visiting the classic place of renovatio: Dante's Purgatorio. Klein, following Dante, writes of the dead there (who are moving toward salvation) as if they were also developing as architects; at first projecting images identical to the self into space and eventually using imagination to design new forms and spaces.

The soul separated from the body by death creates, through its virtù formativa, a new body that resembles the one it had during its lifetime, but whose matter consists of the "surrounding air" of the place of its punishment. This aerial body or "shadow" may not be a spiritus phantasticus in the strict meaning of the term, since it is only created or formed after the death of the subject; but their subtle matters are similar, their spectral natures are identical, and they have the same origin. [...] Moreover, the aerial body Dante attributes to the damned [sic] also characterises Neoplatonic demons — so malleable, Porphyry claims, that they become what they imagine. This is exactly the teaching of Statius's soul in Purgatory — "According as the desires and the other affections prick us, the shade takes its form" (Purgatory, XXV, 106 - 107) — a characteristic which, needless to say, is perfectly suited to the substance of a spiritus phantasticus.[71]

wrecks what it makes known, burning the thought which thinks it and yet requiring this thought in the conflagration where transcendence, immanence are no longer anything but flamboyant, extinguished figures — reference points of writing which writing has always lost in advance. For writing excludes the limitless, continuous process just as much as it seems to include a nonmanifest fragmentation — which in its turn, however, presupposes a continuous surface upon which it would be inscribed, just as it presupposes the experience with which it breaks. Thus, writing continues by discontinuity; it is the lure of silence which, in very absence, has already delivered us to the disastrous return. Intensity: the attractiveness in this name lies not only in its generally escaping conceptualisation, but also its way of coming apart in a plurality of names, de-nominations which dismiss the power that can be exerted as well as the intentionality that orients, and also sign and sense, and the space that unfolds and the time that expatiates. But along with all of this comes some confusion, for intensity's name seems to restore a sort of corporeal interiority — vital vibrancy — whereby the faded teachings of consciousness-unconsciousness are imprinted anew. Whence the necessity to say that only exteriority, in its absolute separation, its infinite disintensification, returns to intensity the disastrous attractiveness that keeps it from letting itself be translated into revelation — a surplus of knowledge, of belief — and turns it back into thought, but thought which exceeds itself and is no longer anything but the torment — the tortuousness — of this return." (Blanchot, op cit, pp.56-57.)

[63] *Joan Copjec, Read My Desire: Lacan against the Historicists, The MIT Press, Cambridge, Mass. and London, 1994, pp.41-42.*

[64] *On 'brain-mind', see J. Allan Hobson, The Chemistry of Conscious States: How the Brain Changes its Mind, Little, Brown & Co., Boston, New York, London, Toronto, 1994. I*

am indebted to Hein and Elma Wagenfeld for this reference.

[65] Copjec, op cit, loc cit.

[66] Ibid., loc cit; Klein, op cit, p.190.

[67] So much for the mislooking committee.

[68] Blanchot, op cit, p.128.

[69] Cf. ibid., p.126.

[70] Trans. from Sigmund Freud, Neue Folge der Vorlesung zur Einführung in die Psychoanlyse. (1933), in his Gesammelte Werke: Chronologisch Geordnet (18 vols, Imago, London, 1940-41, Vol.XV, p.86.

[71] Klein, op cit, p.67.

[72] Ibid., p.81.

[73] Neumeyer, op cit, pp.160-61.

[74] "Indeed, in medieval jurisprudence, 'style' had drifted farther away from its older rhetorical associations and had become a pragmatic means of identifying or authenticating legal documents: the maintenance of a formal or procedural standard protected the document against forgery. It provided the document with a provenance. The historical link to a place and time of execution, in other words, was forged on the mechanical level of legal procedure, or even of penmanship. This was also the function of the clerk's paraph or flourish, an abstract and unrepeatable signature meant to link the document with a particular hand and to foil counterfeiters. This recalls the old sense of style as 'title or appellation'. Falstaff, for example, exclaimed: 'Ford's a knave, and I will aggravate his style'. The usage is ancient in English, but survives today only in the phrase 'self-styled'". (Wood, op cit, p.62.)

[75] Gottfried Semper, The Four Elements of Architecture and Other Writings, trans. Harry Francis Mallgrave and Wolfgang Hermann, Cambridge University Press, Cambridge, 1989, p.39.

[76] Colin Rowe, "Mannerism and Modern Architecture" (1950), in The Mathematics of the Ideal Villa and Other Essays (1976), The MIT Press, Cambridge, Mass. and London, fifth paperback printing 1988, p.45.

[77] That "abstract" view that is unable to see all of Building 8 is co-extensive with Copjec's notion of

the occlusion of physical parts of the (female) hysteric: "The fact that she is constructed by society's language means to the hysteric that parts of her body will not be visible, or present to her". (Copjec, op cit, p.51. Her italics.) Felicia McCarren has argued that this invisibility was present, for both performer and audience, in the quasi-hysterical dances of Loie Fuller: "Fuller's images [...] become seemingly disconnected from any body and require a suspension of disbelief about their origin. Mallarmé describes the viewing her dance requires as a prolonged looking-through, rather than looking at: 'Yes, the suspense of the Dance, contradictory fear or desire to see too much and not enough, requires a transparent prolonging'. Zeroing in on the dance audience's fetishistic or voyeuristic drive to see, Mallarmé describes the site of viewing in terms that psychoanalysis would later familiarise: the contrary fear, or desire that threatens vision with 'too much' or 'not enough'". (Felicia McCarren, "The 'Symptomatic Act' Circa 1900: Hysteria, Hypnosis, Electricity, Dance", Critical Inquiry, Vol. XXI, No.4, Summer 1995, p.757. She cites from Stéphane Mallarmé, Crayonné au théâtre in his Oeuvres complètes, ed. Henri Mondor [1945, Paris, 1984], p.313.) In Space, Time, and Architecture, Harvard University Press, Cambridge, Mass, 1941, pp.494-95, Siegfried Giedion, as Evans points out, publishes reproductions of Picasso's "L'Arlésienne" (1912-13) and Gropius' Bauhaus, both exhibiting what Giedion claimed to be planarity, transparency, and simultaneity. (Evans, op cit, pp.57-58.) Giedion does not offer the "abstract" view discussed by Rowe, but an exposure of both painting and building through the strategies of cubism. In the reproductions, painting and building are more like the hysteric and Loie Fuller; material objects soliciting an apprehension of a wished-for prolonged transparency, up to a point where the transparent vanishes into the material. If anything, Giedion's juxtaposition reveals the occluding tendencies of cubism. Evans notes that there exists (it has been rebuilt) one Gropius work that is "solid but triangular and fractured", the Weimar

This last is aura and cladding of a non-identical entirety. According to Klein, Dante, in the Vita Nuova, in finding the words to praise Beatrice and, in doing so, shows that "the awakening and ascension of the soul has taken place", has included her in the statement of equivalence made by Aquinas and wielded by Mies — adaequatio intellectus et rei.[72] Mies forsook his "forthright theory of 1926 that saw building art as the result of treatment of material and response to function" when his spirituality was awakened by J. J. P. Oud's statement "'Style' always presupposes a spiritual order, that is, a spiritual willing", and Mies's own vita nuova was marked by an enthusiastic embrace of what he termed "the will to the spiritual", "without which beauty [...] was inconceivable", without which the beloved would remain unpraised, and the symbol would not ascend into the invisible.[73]

The symbol does not ascend in Building 8. The building's exterior symbolic force — its style —[74] is at least threefold: its fenestration and the west facade (of mottled and black South Australian basalt with pink squares rotated forty-five degrees and blue-green enigmatic pendant sections set flush with the wall) produce reflections of supplements, its environs — sky, and streetscapes — and inhabitants, passers-by, and traffic, the reflections themselves are themselves a fragmented non-identical entirety; its tiled, clad (both often in diaper patterns), brick, polychromy performs as the supplement to materiality, as a glowing aura, and thus enables the consequent valorisation of form and idea, the "spiritualisation" of materia into res proposed by Gottfried Semper,[75] perhaps the dancers and singers of the intermezzi becoming a hovering, projected space of dance and song; and the large number of facades, all non-identical (eg, the glass veil of the angled south-east facade, and the bleak primal self-identity pushed out into the "surrounding air" by the almost completely unrelieved concrete facing and regular fenestration of so much of the east facade, a "place of punishment", with the rakish overhanging extrusion as a sudden monstration of a spiritus phantasticus), together with the terraces, the three kinds of fire stairs (internal, external, and a buttress-like [or buttress-aping] brick tower with oculi that combines and confronts the qualities of the two other kinds — is its moment in or out?) and variations in the roof, enforce a comprehension of an entirety that is not intelligible as a single building but as a virtual town or a sociogenic event, not even what Colin Rowe calls the "non-visual angle, the 'abstract' view from the air" that make Gropius's Dessau Bauhaus (1926-27) coherent[76] would be able to show all of it.[77]

On reflections:

A metonymy and manners for the reflected if they see themselves: at the conclusion of the "Pageant" of local and national history the performance of which is the spine of Virginia Woolf's novel Between The Acts a surprise is sprung on the audience:

Look! Out they come, from the bushes — the riff-raff. Children? Imps — elves — demons. Holding what? Tin cans? Bed-room candlesticks? Old jars? My dear, that's the cheval glass from the Rectory! And the mirror — that I lent her. My mother's. Cracked. What's the notion? Anything that's bright enough to reflect, presumably, ourselves?

Ourselves! Ourselves!

Out they leapt, jerked, skipped. Flashing, dazzling, dancing, jumping. Now old Bart...he was caught. Now Manresa. Here a nose...There a skirt...Then trousers only...Now perhaps a face...Ourselves? But that's cruel. To snap us as we are, before we've had time to assume...And only, too, in parts...That's what's so distorting and upsetting and utterly unfair.
[...]
Look at ourselves, ladies and gentlemen! Then at the wall; and ask how's this wall, the great wall, which we call, perhaps miscall, civilisation, to be built by (here the mirrors flicked and flashed) orts, scraps and fragments like ourselves?

[...]
The gramophone was affirming in tones that there was no denying, triumphant yet valedictory: Dispersed are we; who have come together. But, the gramophone asserted let us maintain whatever made that harmony.[78]

Blanchot writes on the death of Narcissus:
What is mythical in this myth is death's practically unnamed presence — in the water, in the spring, in the flowery shimmering of a limpid enchantment which does not open onto the frightfully unfathomable underground, but reflects it dangerously (crazily) in the illusion of a surface proximity.[79]

In his "place of punishment", Narcissus is advanced into a renovatio; he and his site become the designed emanation of a spiritus phantasticus. Other emanations operate as reflections of a destabilising entirety in the reflective silver leaf which Brunelleschi framed his perspective drawing of the Baptistery in Florence: the viewer, in the camera obscura of this assemblage, would have seen how, virtually, the environment acted upon the image and how the image acted upon the environment; the viewer would have seen a virtual environmental design. As Hubert Damisch writes:

[...T]his way of mirroring that he inserted into the pictorial field like a piece of marquetry and onto which the sky and its clouds were captured, this mirror is thus much more than a subterfuge. It has the value of an epistemological emblem [...] to the extent to which it reveals the limitations of the perspective code, for which the demonstration furnishes the complete theory. It makes perspective appear as a structure of exclusions, whose coherence is founded on a series of refusals that nonetheless must make a place, as the background onto which it is printed, for the very thing it excludes from its order.[80]

Here the supplements inflect, do not infect, the building.

Kapp-Putsch Monument (1920-22).
(Evans, op cit, p.67.) I do not believe the
"abstract" view or the "transparent prolonging"
will ever be able to fix this poignant, aspiring, yet
imprecating, crumpling yet consoling, thing.

78 Virginia Woolf, Between The Acts (1941),
Ace Books, London, 1961, pp.117, 120, 126.

79 Blanchot, op cit, p.126.

80 Hubert Damisch, Theorie du/nuage/, Editions
du Seuil, Paris, 1972, pp.170-71. Cited and
trans. in Rosalind Krauss, "The Grid, The/
Cloud/, and The Detail", in The Presence of
Mies, ed. Detlef Mertins, Princeton Architectural
Press, New York, 1994, p.142.

81 Bois, op cit, p.60.

82 Gottfried Semper, Der Stil in den technischen
und tektonischen Künsten, Vol.I (Frankfurt,
1860), § 76, p.445. Cited and trans. in Kruft,
op cit, p.315; and in Semper, The Four Elements,
p.39.

83 "Going for the Good: Recent Work by
Peter Corrigan", interview with Corrigan by
Marcus O'Donnell, Monument, No.8, p.4.

84 Cf. Rowe, op cit, pp.29-57.

85 Rilke, Duino Elegies, pp.84-85. Translation
modified.

86 Copjec, op cit, p.54. Her italics.

87 Yates, The Rosicrucian Enlightenment,
Routledge & Kegan Paul, London, 1972,
frontispiece and p.93.

88 Semper, The Four Elements, pp.255-56.

89 In discussing Walter Benjamin's idea of each
epoch dreaming the next, and simultaneously
reconstructing the one before (Benjamin,
Baudelaire: A Lyric Poet in the Era of High
Capitalism ["Das Paris des Second Empire bei
Baudelaire" and "Über einige Motive von
Baudelaire", 1938-39], trans. Harry Zohn, New
Left Books, London, 1973, p.176), Douglas
Crimp states: "There is no simple Now: every
present is non-synchronous, a mix of different
times'". (Crimp, "Postmodernism in Parallax",
October, 63, Winter 1993.) This is Semper's
now, and that of Building 8. For an extensive
discussion of Benjamin and now-in-time, see
Missac, op cit, pp.83-123.

90 "I should like to persuade sensible people and
sensible historians to use the word Rosicrucian.
This word has bad associations owing to the
uncritical assertions of occultists concerning the
existence of a secret society or sect calling
themselves Rosicrucians, the history and
membership of which they claim to establish.
Though it is important that the arguments for and
against a Rosicrucian society should be carefully
and critically sifted, I should like to use the word
here without raising the secret society question at
all. [...I]t might then come to designate a phase in
the history of the Hermetic tradition in relation to
science. [...] The influx of Paracelsan alchemy and
medicine, itself originally stimulated by Ficinian
influences, is important for [...] the Rosicrucian
type, who is often, perhaps always, strongly
influenced by Paracelsus. The tradition in its later
or Rosicrucian phase begins to become imbued with
philanthropic aims, possibly as a result of
Paracelsan influence. [...T]he situation of the
Rosicrucian in society is worse and more
dangerous than that of the earlier magi. [...] The
Rosicrucian [...] tends to have persecution mania."
(Yates, "The Hermetic Tradition in Renaissance
Science" [1967], in Collected Essays, 3 vols,
Routledge & Kegan Paul, London, Boston,
Melbourne and Henley, 1982-84, Vol.III,
pp.234-35.)

91 Yates, The Rosicrucian Enlightenment, p.94.

92 This is probably a Protestant summons,
warning, an Appel, to Catholic Counter-
Reformation Rome, south-west of the Bohemia in
which the College seems to trundle.
Cf. Hans Pfitzner's opera (Musikalische Legende)
Palestrina (1915), in which the musical motif
denoting "Rome" is an ostinato, a ringing,
throbbing, metrical unconscious, which augments
and swells after the legendary one night
composition of the Missa Papae Marcelli by
Palestrina (a composition, begged for Borromeo
and, even, by the ghosts of dead composers, among
whom are Josquin Desprez and Enrico Tedesco)
that mediates polyphony into the "placet" and yeas
of the anti-polyphonic factions of the legates of
Pope Pius IV and most of the Council of Trent);

On supplements:

Bois has pointed out that Derrida, in Of Grammatology, devotes a long passage "to the supplementary nature of colour in Western aesthetics".[81] Semper was aware of this supplementarity of colour; he named it Bekleidung ("cladding" or "dressing") and was also aware of its once-operant, and potential power to exalt form over material, manner over matter. As he writes:

[...T]he emancipation of form from the grasp of the material and from brute necessity [...] Following this tendency, the Hellenic building principle had to vindicate and nourish colour as the subtlest, most bodiless coating. It was the most perfect means to do away with reality, for while it dressed the material, it was itself immaterial. It also corresponded in other respects to the freer tendencies of Hellenic Art.[82]

In an interview, Peter Corrigan talked about his "poor architecture": "It's basically bang for the buck. An attempt to dignify modest resources. There seems to be a 'good' in solving problems with modest resources".[83] Building 8 is a polychromatic mannerism[84] stretched and strapped for cash, in which the "poor" materials act (Tun), according to their indwelling abilities in acting so that, as matter, they appear to dissemble, and also according to the manners of their designed disposition, as a dilating promise (almost a presence) of an immanent abundance at the moments of its flowering and blazoning out of itself, as an "unlimited field of poetic achievements", an aletheia:

Tun unter Krusten, die willig zerspringen, sobald innen das Handeln entwächst und sich anders begrenzt. (Act under crusts, that will readily burst open as soon as the inner action outgrows them and takes a different outline.)[85]

Copjec would interrogate this: "Since signifiers are not transparent, they cannot demonstrate that they are not hiding something behind what they say — they cannot prove that they do not lie."[86]

At least two buildings come to mind as supplements to, impinging on, and appearing over, Building 8: one, polychromatic, is proposed by Semper; the other, polysemic yet an entirety, The Invisible College of the Rose Cross Fraternity, by someone who, using the name Theophilus Schweighardt, in 1618 published a tract called Speculum Sophicum Rhodo-Stauroticum (The Mirror of the Wise Rosicrucians) together with which the print of the College was bound.[87] Semper advances:

The festival apparatus, the improvised scaffolding with all the special splendour and frills that indicate more precisely the occasion for the festivity and enhance the glorification of the day — covered with decorations, draped with carpets, dressed with boughs and flowers, adorned with festoons and garlands, fluttering banners and trophies — this is the motive of the permanent monument, which is intended to recount for coming generations the festive act and the event celebrated. Thus the Egyptian temple arose from the motive of the improvised pilgrim's market [...][88]

This supplement is not a historicist recollection; but rather, a wish for a non-deferred sociability in Semper's now.[89]

The Invisible College is an emblem for behaving in an ethical way in a bloody time: that is its motive.[90] It, however, does not possess only a motive but is also motile, a symbolised idea, behind and before the emblem, traversing (and desiring to transfigure) the world. The College is presented as a rusticated block form with three visible bartizans, dome, lantern, and bell-cote, mounted on wheels, and pulled in a northerly direction by a hand thrust through a cloud. Two square windows allow us to see a scholar pondering a globe, a vase of flowers (perhaps medicinal herbs) and what appear to be architectural models or scientific instruments. On either side of the central arched doorway are anaglyphs of a rose and a cross. From the building a giant arm and hand are thrust, brandishing a sword labelled Cavete ("beware") towards the north-east where Noah's ark is

balanced on its mountain, a trumpet labelled "C.R.F". (Yates suggest this is an abbreviation of "Christian Rosenkreutz Frater", the mythical founder of the invisible order)[91] sounds out a call for renovatio to the south-west.[92] Three men waving wings and bearing shields with the Name of God blazoned on them stand in the bartizans, and pairs of wings carrying letters addressed to Fratres fly along appointed courses. *"In the sky, to the left and right of the central name and wings, are a Serpent and a Swan, bearing stars, and alluding to the 'new stars' in Serpentarius [the constellation named the Serpent-Bearer] and Cygnus [the Swan...] prophetic of a new dispensation".* [93]

The fragmentary and chaotic description above, which elides some signifiers Yates knows and also some I know, is not written in the "slow agony of reference" but in a grab for efflorescing and protuberant forms and meanings. The take is surfed, not constructed. The College is an apparition of renovatio as a supplement from the invisible and virtual now, a Kleistian nostalgia,[94] not secured in that invisible: "[...W]e have not the utopia of this moment but the care of its potential".[95]

On the Town:

In basic narratological studies a work of fiction has at least two operations: a plot, that is, what happens, and an emplotment, an exposure or occlusion of where what happens happens. In Hardy's The Mayor of Casterbridge,[96] by the time the plot is over, through the emplotment we have been given a complete set of exterior approaches to and apertures of the town; and also we have read of the "cladding" of the keys that Mother Cuxsom attributes to those articles of the dead Susan Henchard ("And all her shining keys will be took from her")[97] In this image Mother Cuxsom "re-ignites the glimmer of hope in the past";[98] of the supplement (the landscape) apprehended *an ostinato, before which, both in affection and defiance, ambivalently in concord and discord with, so contiguous with, which — yet apart from, and against it — thus enacting an Academical preconscious, Palestrina's pupil, Silla, sings a secular song — a conscious, if halting, erotic address to a pagan nymph; after Act One, Silla disappears from the stage, having gone to join Bardi in Florence. In the opera, Silla's song is a future renovatio still to be completed; Palestrina's mass, a present renovatio that is a coagulation and redemption of the past. On the Italian Academies, see Yates, "The Italian Academies" (1949), in Collected Essays, ed cit, Vol.II, pp.6-29.*

[93] *Yates, The Rosicrucian Enlightenment, loc cit.*

[94] *"Kleist's nostalgia for the marionette is a nostalgia for the man still interwoven with the cosmos, of which Plato spoke in the Laws, an ensemble of cords and interior strings by means of which the gods lead and guide this man. In the marionette is preserved the memory of the golden chain that once united the universe with indissoluble links." (Cacciari, op cit, p.185.) For more on the "chain", see Roberto Calasso, The Marriage of Cadmus and Harmony (Le Nozze di Cadmo ed Armonia, 1988), trans. Tim Parks, Jonathan Cape, London, 1993, passim; and my "Ether, Net, Dust Mound, or Red Mountain", Object, No.2, 1995, pp.32-35. In Pfitzner's opera, Palestrina apostrophises God, requesting him to recognise that he, the composer, has forged — through his composition, the renovatio — the last link in the golden chain of polyphony, and has made the chain operant again.*

[95] *Cacciari, op cit, p.174. His italics.*

[96] *Winner of the 1863 silver medal from the R.I.B.A. for his essay "On the Application of Coloured Bricks and Terra Cotta to Modern Architecture" (although he did not receive the £10 money prize that accompanied it); and project director, following G. R. Crickmay's plans, of the Green Hill Housing Estate, Weymouth (1871) where he put his polychromy into practice. See Robert Gittings, Young Thomas Hardy, Heinemann, London, 1975, pp.65, 68, 152-53.*

[97] *Hardy, The Mayor of Casterbridge (1886, 1912), p.142.*

[98] *Cacciari, op cit, p.146.*

[99] *Hardy, The Mayor, p.146.*

[100] *Ibid., op cit, p.144.*

[101] *It is published as plate 4 in Jörg C. Kirschenmann and Eberhard Syring, Hans Scharoun: Die Förderung des Unvollendeten, Deutsche Verlags-Anstalt, Stuttgart, 1993, p.169. It is also reproduced in colour in Peter Blundell Jones, Hans Scharoun, Phaidon, London, 1995, p.105.*

[102] *John Ruskin, The Stones of Venice, II, The Sea-Stories, in The Works, Library Edition, eds. E. T. Cook and A. Wedderburn, 39 vols, George Allen, London, 1903-12, Vol.X, p.83.*

[103] *Ibid., The Queen of the Air, in ed cit, Vol.XIX, pp.360-61. His italics.*

[104] *Ibid., ed cit, Vol.XIX, pp.362-63.*

[105] *Ibid., ed cit, loc cit. Yet, cf. the studied but still gainsaying (through Nachträglichkeit, the arrested movement of an abiding yet deferred world-motion) velocity of the Serpent in Coleridge's "Psyche" (1805, published 1834), in which aerial aspiration is focused in the Greek for "butterfly" and "soul" (psyche): "[...] For in this earthly frame/Ours is the reptile's lot, much toil, much blame,/Manifold motions making little speed,/And to deform and kill the things whereon we feed." (See Samuel Taylor Coleridge, Selected Poetry and Prose, ed. Donald A. Stauffer, Random House, New York, 1951, pp.4, 153.) This Serpent is as vicious as that of Ruskin's prestidigitator ("Look! No hands!"), but its habitat is more viscid, presented in a "manifold" entropy.*

[106] *Ibid., ed cit, Vol.X, p.341.*

[107] *Conrad Hamann, Cities of Hope:*

from afar as Henchard stares through the frame of the letter written by Susan that denies his paternity of Elizabeth-Jane ("Her husband regarded the letter as if it were a window-pane through which he saw for miles"); [99] and we have been penetrated by the supplement, again, the landscape, introjecting itself into the interior ("Henchard [...] moving like a great tree in the wind").[100]

I have not eased Klein's dilemma of an entire space so packed with divergent symbols and meanings that analysis is in agony and/or becomes aphasic. I have only practiced some typology, metonymy and iconography on the exteriors of Building 8. Now two knots or assemblages and their relation are to be briefly scanned: the building's exterior and interior.

3. CLOUD/BIRD/WAVE AND SERPENT

There exists a watercolour and pencil visionary sketch design drawn by Scharoun, working as, and in his, spiritus phantasticus, during World War II.[101] It indicates at some distance a vast public building with double staircases crossing hexagonally in elevation, a mounting approach of Piranesian depth receding from the foreground along what is either a wall that is not so much a veil as a boulevard of cyclopean, massed, positive space or another cyclopean construction, a heavily rendered rectilinear building, over all of which flies a roof of six clouds or tidal waves, which fan out exposing (I suppose) the huge void of the interior to the immense haecceities of the sky. One looks at this populated yet uncrowded sheet and learns something about the necessity to put the visionary into discourse (evidence of loss and restropective hope of rebuilding or of building a new res). No other architectural sketch, to my mind, has evoked such an admixture of delicacy, intimacy, immensity, and sociogenesis. This sketch was part of his project to locate and mobilise the supplement to the war. The cloud/wave-forms of the roof of Building 8 are more economical, urban rather than universal and utopian. The characteristic images that Ruskin's aerial imagination was expressed in were the wave — he saw the highest horizon line of them all — ("*as if in ecstasy, the crests of the arches break into marble foam, and toss themselves far into the blue sky in flashes and wreaths of sculptured spray, as if the breakers on the Lido shore had been frost-bound before they fell, and the sea-nymphs had inlaid them with coral and amethyst*"),[102] and the cloud/bird: ("*upon the plumes of the bird are put the colours of the air: on these the gold of the cloud, that cannot be gathered by any covetousness; the rubies of the clouds, that are not the price of Athena, but are Athena; the vermilion of the cloud-bar, and the flame of the cloud-crest, and the snow of the cloud, and its shadow, and the melted blue of the deep wells of the sky — all these, seized by the creating spirit, and woven by*

Athena herself into films and threads of plume; with wave on wave following and fading along breast, and throat, and opened wings, infinite as the dividing of the foam and the sifting of the sea-sand; — even the white down of the cloud seeming to flutter up between the stronger plumes, seen, but too soft for touch"). [103] How sea-like is his sky! His recurring earthbound nightmare was the serpent ("*There are myriads lower than this and more loathsome, in the scale of being; the links between dead matter and animation drift everywhere unseen. But it is the strength of the base element that is so dreadful in the serpent: it is of the very omnipotence of the earth. [...] As the bird is the clothed power of the air, so this is the clothed power of the dust; as the bird the symbol of the spirit of life, so this of the grasp and sting of death."*)[104] He is most troubled by being unable to determine its manner of moving: "I cannot understand this swift forward motion of serpents".[105] In The Stones of Venice, Ruskin claims not to be able to see within the Ducal Palace, the "extremity, wherein lay the sting and force of the whole creature [...] the serpent, which is the type of eternity", and defers into that infinity the vision of "the Palace Serpent".[106] It soon becomes clear yet besmirching that this Serpent could be the symbol of the invisible and motile System operating in, but not designing, some of the interiors (eg, the Level 2 lobby [which is all of a type with the "blowzy, noisy, sprawling space" that Conrad Hamann sees as the interior of the Andrews building],[107] offices, and teaching spaces) in Building 8. The System might be travestied but, according to Blanchot, travesty is truly its re-reinforcement : "So it is that the travesty of the System — the System raised by irony to an absolute of absoluteness — is a way for the System still to impose itself by the discredit with which the demand of the fragmentary credits it".[108] Forster writes on Mrs Moore's experience of a Marabar cave:

Australian Architecture and Design by Edmond and Corrigan 1962-92, Oxford University Press, Melbourne, 1993, p.139.

[108] *Blanchot, op cit, p.61.*

[109] *Forster, op cit, p.203.*

[110] *Evans, op cit, p.21.*

[111] *Cf. Richard Thorp, of Mitchell, Giurgola, Thorp, on the interiors of the New Parliament (1988) in Canberra: "[I]n a real sense the building didn't cost very much [...] this is a huge building. It is the correct price per square metre and everything. A few areas have materials above the norm. The majority of the building is made of plasterboard and metal ceiling tiles and carpeted floors, the same as any office building". (Cited in James Weirick, "Don't You Believe It: Critical Response to the New Parliament House", Transition, Nos.27/28, Summer/Autumn 1989, p.55.)*

[112] *Benjamin, One-Way Street, p.78. Translation modified. "[...I] lay stretched out in bed, my eyes staring upwards, my nostrils flaring, my heart beating; until habit had changed the colour of the curtains, silenced the clock, brought an expression of pity to the cruel slanting face of the glass, disguised or even completely dispelled the scent of vetiver, and appreciably had reduced the height of the ceiling. Habit! that skilful but slow-moving arranger who begins by letting our minds suffer for weeks on end in temporary quarters, but whom our minds are none the less happy to discover at last, for without it, reduced to their own devices, they would be powerless to make any room habitable." (Proust, Swann's Way, op cit, Vol.I, pp.8-9.)*

[113] *Michel de Certeau, The Practice of Everyday Life (Arts de faire, 1974), trans. Stephen Rendall, University of California Press, Berkeley and Los Angeles, first paperback printing 1988, pp.25-26. His italics.*

[114] *Theodor W. Adorno, Negative Dialectics, trans. E. B. Ashton, Routledge & Kegan Paul, London, 1973, p.160.*

115 Rilke, Duino Elegies, p.24. Translation modified.

116 See n.6, above.

117 See n.5, above.

118 Hardy, The Return of the Native (1878, 1912), pp.83, 376.

119 G. W. F. Hegel, Phenomenology of Spirit (Phänomenologie des Geistes, 1807), trans. A. V. Miller, Oxford University Press, Oxford, paperback edition 1979, p.423. Miller's italics.

120 Blanchot, op cit, p. 142.

121 See ns. 14 and 15, above.

122 Tafuri and Francesco Dal Co, Modern Architecture (1976), trans. Robert Erich Wolf, 2 vols, Faber & Faber, London; Electa Editrice, Milan, paperback edition 1986, Vol.2, p.255. I am indebted to Leon van Schaik for the reference to Aalto.

123 Evans, op cit, p.74. My italics.

124 Ibid., loc cit.

125 Rowe, op cit, p.45.

126 Camillo Sitte, City Planning According to Artistic Principles (Der Städtebau, 1899), cited and trans. in George R. Collins and Christiane Crasemann Collins, Camillo Sitte: The Birth of Modern City Planning, Rizzoli, New York, 1986, p.249.

127 "The spirit of masks breathes in Shakespeare's dramas; we meet the humour of masks and the haze of candles, the carnival sentiment (which truly is not always joyous) in Mozart's Don Juan. [...] Masking does not help, however, when behind the mask the thing is false or the mask is no good." (Semper, The Four Elements, p.257. The italics are his.) Cf.,also, "[...T]he old Spanish play, entitled Atheista Fulminato, formerly, and perhaps still, acted in the churches and monasteries of Spain, and which, under various names (Don Juan, the Libertine, etc.) has had its day of favour in every country throughout Europe. A popularity so extensive, and of a work so grotesque and extravagant, claims

"Boum, it amounts to the same. Visions are supposed to entail profundity, but — Wait till you get one, dear reader! The abyss also may be petty, the serpent of eternity made of maggots [...]".[109] Evans writes on the "diabolocentric" cosmos of medieval and early Renaissance imaginings: "The centre was corrupt, as in a maggoty apple, and man's eccentric, superficial position was uncongenial, estranged and full of yearning or distraction".[110] In the failed interiors [111] three things might occur: (1) their occupants introject the constructive manifold force of the exteriors into them and charge, as after-images, as scintillating zones for behaviour, the "surrounding air" with that force, that "new dispensation"; (2) the occupants fall prey to Benjamin's Proustian "Habit" — which makes what is sensed and lost in space impalpable and replaced — ("*As soon as we begin to find our bearings, the landscape vanishes at a stroke like the façade of a house as we enter it. It has not yet gained preponderance [because it is exhausted by] a constant exploration that has become habit.*");[112] or (3) the occupants take up the common French tactic recorded by Michel de Certeau as la perruque in which "[the worker] cunningly takes pleasure in finding a way to create gratuitous products whose sole purpose is to signify his own capabilities and to confirm his solidarity with other workers [...] through spending his time in this way",[113] in other words, through improvisation and discreet intervention they re-design what is forlorn in the strategy of the System. The non-identity of two terms, "exteriors/some public interiors" and "offices/ teaching areas" is idling in a reciprocal negativity. Adorno writes: "*What is negated, is negative until it has past. This is the decisive break with Hegel*".[114] The (as yet) abiding negatives — death in the Purgatorio — are enacted in the transition from the exteriors to the interior of Building 8: figured in the after-images blasted on the blindness of Rilke's angel (in the blindnesses of the System of all his angels the poet cries out "Wer, wenn ich schriee, hörte mich denn aus der Engel/Ordnungen?" ["Who, if I cried out,

would hear me out of/from/amongst the Angelic Orders?"]),[115] figured in Narcissus shutting his eyes and prey to after-images of himself and the other, even Echo (he would state "Dispossession possessed me", he becomes the would-be errant Atlas at the moment of being tricked into bearing the System again,[116] a conformity),[117] and figured in the muting, the silence, the plot and emplotment, having passed through the façade, of the dead woman, once "sauntering", raking into and against her environment, reflective, supplementary, and place-making, of the spatial limner, a metonymy of architecture parlante, Eustacia Vye of Hardy's The Return of the Native: "The expression of her finely carved mouth was pleasant, as if a sense of dignity had just compelled her to leave off speaking".[118] That "sense of dignity" is death for her, for Building 8 it is the System. In Hegel's argument, which makes Adorno's "break" not as "decisive" as he claims, the System's primal state was purely matter, a petrified "inner being" that Nature, worked by artificers, hid away like a fetish: "*Over against this outer shape of the self [that 'needs the rays of the sun in order to have sound, which generated by light, is even then merely noise and not speech', an architecture sonore, perhaps like Rilke's Ur-Geräusch, primal sound, produced by traversing the coronal suture with a gramophone needle] stands the other shape which proclaims its possession of an inner being. Nature, withdrawing into its essence [a symbol in the invisible as proposed by Cacciari], deposes its living, self-particularising, self-entangling manifold existence to the level of an inessential husk [the aim of cladding], which is the covering for the inner being; and this inner being is, in the first instance, still simple darkness, the unmoved, the black, formless stone*".[119] As it develops, the System retains its formlessness but attains structure. It is a stratification without substance. Yet, within the interior of Building 8, there are forms that have come in like great trees and resist the System's breezes and blasts. The ogee moulding that is realised, and blossoms, at the east termination of the stairway between levels 4 and 5 is an amalgam of Ruskin's beloved Gothic and the forms developed in Spain by and between the Islamic and Sephardic peoples before their expulsion from Spain: it is a felt type of, prompting an ideational dilation of the amalgam into, what Blanchot advances as l'epokhe[120] a time more future, that is, expanding toward an enriched, abundant, augmented future in which the amalgam would operate in a redeemed plenitude (in the stairs' descent the ogee augments their flight), Messianic time. It is another geometrical and artfully deliquescent, expanding, yet without loss of the arborescent curving — the organic dead superposed as formal delight — (a spiritus phantasticus would be discerned, or emanate out, of the tree), sign of Sullivan's perilous and longed for triad, the 'grammar of ornament based on organic (embryonic) and inorganic (geometric) basic forms, in which through the overlapping of divisions and expansions, human power shows itself in action."[121] The Aalto-like polychromatic tiled columns placed close to the stairs and escalators are markers of physical (not academic) ascent: they embody Aalto's "abstract organicism" in which his "hermetic accents" abide yet from which his "cordiality" has been elided.[122] Aalto, in his design for the Jyväskylä University Model Primary School (1950-56), as Evans suggests and Aalto himself confesses, was, like Edmond & Corrigan, unable to bounce out the System: "*The school remains administratively one, while made several in appearance and imagination*".[123] Aalto camouflages the Serpent and sweetens its habitat. "*[The] subdivision [of his spaces] is an emollient that softens the outline of authority, reduces the appearance of power. [...] As the scale decreases and the definition increases, it presses in on available space, eventually imposing the free impulses it was meant to release. When Louis Kahn was asked why he did not make buildings like Aalto, he replied that a building composed of designed responses to casual activity would be a monument; it would monumentalise casualness,*

freezing and preserving the ephemeral activity that other monuments left unspecified. [...] Architects such as Aalto were obliged to steer between the Scylla of overdeterminate differentiation at a smaller scale and the Charybdis of indeterminate differentiation at a larger scale".[124] Kahn points out the potential of a regression to the black stone. Building 8 is the Wandering Rocks of overdeterminate differentiation at a larger scale. In its more winding spaces it performs the designed labyrinth Rowe anticipated without much enthusiasm in 1950,[125] and Camillo Sitte had scorned as a "*fabricated ingenuousness [...] on the drawing board*" in 1899.[126] Fabrication of the ersatz is not a renewal on which a future can be founded. Renovatio: if only the Serpent would slough its inside and the Bird would take roost in there and the Cloud drift in and the Wave break. Building 8 is at present a collage: one entirety forged out of the non-identicality of its elements (the manifold of the res) masking[127] one disfigured, discontinuous area of internal and systemised, rarely shored up or designed (as in compartition) fragments (the aphasia and aporia of the materia); both entirety and area are accidental supplements, torn together (without a working or, even, a interrogated, transgressed adaequatio — the interrogation and transgression of which seems to have been the origin and goal of each and every and always failing and failed renovatio), enacting Max Ernst's perverse and unsettling Entortung, attack on place: "*the coupling of two realities, irreconcilable in appearance, upon a place which apparently does not suit them*".[128]

and merits philosophical attention and investigation. The first point to be noticed is, that the play is throughout imaginative. Nothing of it belongs to the real world, but the names of places and persons. The comic parts, equally with the tragic; the living equally with the defunct characters, are creatures of the brain, as little amenable to the rules of ordinary probability, as the Satan of Paradise Lost or the Caliban of the Tempest, and therefore to be understood as and judged of as impersonated abstractions." (Coleridge, op cit, pp.402-03.)

[128] *Max Ernst, Beyond Painting, Wittenborn and Schultz, New York, 1948, p.13. An Ernst collage, "Adieu mon beau pays de Marie Laurencin" (1919), shows a construction on wheels on which is inscribed the words "MAMAN TOUJOURS FJC-TICK". The Ernst is a perhaps a type of the destroyed Edmond & Corrigan wheeled motile contraption, "Tram Number 567" (1978), which was indited inside with honour boards of the names of personal heroes, the Carlton drinking school, and the Australian Performing Group, scrawled outside with mottoes of a desired renovatio of harmony and renewal ("Sayonara Koala" and "Pasolini Lives"), and in large lettering lengthwise on its sides, it bore a message of simultaneous consolation and menace — "MOTHER KNOWS!".*

Michael Anderson

Building and Theatre:
An Edited Interview with Peter Corrigan

Photograph: Moshe Dinor.

Building 8 could be subjected to an analysis which might configure it in terms of a collection of theatrical tricks: cut screens, layered flattage, dramatic lighting effects, faux curtaining, unfolding spatial narratives, etc. This woud be a way of drawing parallels between the building and stage-design work emanating from the office of Edmond & Corrigan. But it would also be a superficial enterprise, perpetuating traditional notions of theatre by reducing scenography to a series of effects, which uprooted from their "natural" stage environment, can adhere to built form and thereby render it "theatrical".

This interview was constructed around the premise that what links the scenography and architecture of Edmond & Corrigan is an approach, or an underlying set of principles, rather than the application of identifiable tropes.

MA
Given the evolution of your work and the discourse surrounding it, is it becoming more difficult and more complex to situate the work within a discourse?

PC
When I was a student, I remember reading an interview with Mies where he said that he had simply devoted his life to bring order to the human confusion that surrounds us. I remember thinking at the time that this was a shade ambitious and more than a little pompous. This of course was undergraduate ignorance and jealousy, and I've always admired him. Personally, I never believed that architecture simply involved designing buildings. l don't care for that idea. To look at building design as if there was some kind of intrinsic "good", the well-tempered design, well l still don't believe it. Design is not value-free. In a way, as l look at the contemporary work that is applauded, the fatuous design quality of a great deal of it is simply an empty lifestyle quality. Occasionally l wonder how I'm ever going to survive. So working in the theatre is a joy. No one in the theatre believes that what you see is the end of the experience;

there is always a larger proposition, a combination or a series of propositions/ contributions being made. You hope that some humanist or ethical concern or just some slight sense of decency is glimpsed, and that the g.p. leave the theatre marginally better for the experience; or at least possibly they considered it. I don't have any patience with the "supreme uselessness of art" push. There was a time in architecture when hopes and ideals were identified and they were taught. We all know why change occurred and we understand that gravitas is not a characteristic of our time. l sometime wonder (late on Sunday afternoons in the backyard) about the future of the office. I don't see many who are interested in the things that interest me. So, yes, I suppose that qualifies me to be outside the discourse. But it depends on if you play the man or the ball.

It is interesting you should raise the word gravitas in relation to a building that presents a very playful face to the public and one which seems more celebratory than critical. You have, in the past, enunciated a clear position with regard to the relationship between creative activity and social critique: where do you see Building 8 fitting into that landscape of social critique and proposing some form of gravitas?

Well l never doubted that this is a serious building, and l think celebration might be a way into the proposition. In some respects I'm still — and l hope this doesn't sound mawkish — trying to assess what it is I've done. You start off blazing away from position A, B and C and in the end you arrive at X, Y and Z, and try to test or tease out a journey or process through the maze. But certainly celebration has been at the heart of a great deal of it. In terms of building "a society", well, it's that old left-wing notion of the good society. I read something recently about the possibility of the good society, and I'd like to think that's probably what the building might be about: the possibility of the good society.

Not the conclusive description of the good. We might draw a long Lou Kahn bow and say "What might such a building be?" It does seem to me that there could be a worthwhile social or ethical dimension to a design process. The architectural design solution should lead us to an idea, a proposition. It should/might offer a redeeming or at least a consoling myth. Design in the theatre, however, usually enhances some ideas that the audience consider — as a result of buying a ticket. There, design has teeth.

A great deal of what's happening architecturally is design that has taken on its own privilege. Like making jewellery, it has become an inflated craft form. Fortunately, there are architects like Daniel Libeskind who not only talk with some reluctance about design, but who prefer to talk about culture, which I think is extremely moving. Somebody like Dan is a very interesting / important figure; he talks about a larger vision, the human condition, the larger responsibilities. That's really the point — where does the responsibility lie? How do we live with responsibility? How do we carry ethical responsibilities through life? I think these are significant issues, and if these become the informing material for an architecture, well then that architecture might yet fulfil the promise of modernity.

Is there, pervading the architectural mission, a sense of "audience" which carries over from your theatre work? I'd like you to speculate on that, with regard to your comments about the role of Building 8 in promulating a vision or larger idea — that it might map or sketch out a position in relation to an idea. That sort of thinking has a place in the theatre, in terms of construcing a world, constructing a vision, constructiong a set of ideas for the consumption or the speculative possiblities invoked through having an audience present. Is there possibly something of that sort of attitude towards an audience which pervades Building 8?

Oh, certainly; I think the proposition that students go to the building as they might go to the theatre sounds fine. The idea of sitting and watching the building and being forced to make judgements, why it is so, and so on. But the dissidence throughout the building is certainly not artful. The more I look at it, the more I am taken by the enthusiastic clumsiness of certain aspects. I would like to think that this lack of "artifice" may provoke a question or two. In the theatre the ability to provoke the audience to question, is inherent, a responsibility. There is a necessity to provoke query and response. It's not so within architecture. There is the spatial grandeur syndrome that's rooted in classicism. There's "the elegant", "the tense", and "the tough", based on a modernist viewpoint. The present assumption is that architecture never sets out to raise big questions, or even little ones. It simply is of itself, a benign presence in our time.

Well, to draw another parallel between your recent theatre work and Building 8, both realms of operation seem deliberately to set out to resist closure. Perhaps it's through overburdening the stage space with references, suggestions and quotations, indeed, overburdening the stage space with meaning, that it resists closure. It seems to me that there's a similar sort of tactic being pursued in your recent built work.

Yes, I accept that response. There's not much of an attempt here to close down or edit out. I constantly hear that word being bandied around as a hallmark of design. The idea that design is a reductivist procedure, well, I just don't believe it. The notion that "If there are two good equal and opposite ideas, then choose one" never really appealed to me. I still do believe that you choose both. Time and time will be the judge, the Tony Hancock "rich tapestry of life" model.

You find opportunity to pursue a pluralistic approach like this when given a big stage space. With Building 8, you've been given your biggest stage yet; it's your first really big project, although these things are, of course, relative. Looking at your history of stage work, considering productions such as Don Giovanni, Richard II, and now Nabucco, are you able to characterise a sensibility that confronting a big stage, a big production, might trigger off in you? Do you find it more threatening than working in a more intimate space?

No. There is no relationship between the size of the stage and the size of the imaginative grasp of the director. If we press that analogy a little bit, then the imaginative size of the building might be in some relationship to the dreams of the client, the dream and the imaginative capacity of the client. It was a very unusual point in time at RMIT; there was a client who was able to articulate an ambition for the building. I would say that just as working with a director who can confidently cut to the heart of a production is important, so a client right behind the whole project gives a lot of impulse and confidence. And that made a big difference. Scale itself was not an issue — it didn't necessarily magnify the process.

I suppose that what I'm getting at here is something that you said some time ago about fear being the great motivator. And I was wondering whether maybe with an increase in scale there's a corresponding increase in the horreur vacuui. Does the fear of the void increase with the immensity of the project?

No, that's a "sizeist" theory. I think that I started designing this building when I was at Melbourne University. All the time I spent in New York working in all of those offices on large buildings was in preparation for this. So when it happened I didn't have the slightest hesitation. There was no doubt about "how".

To, say, work with Barrie Kosky down in some little art studio in Prahan, and then move straight onto the stage of the Sydney Opera House ... I suppose there's a point where really you either know what you're doing or you don't. As our Prime Minister Paul Keating observed when asked: "Do you watch the TV news?", "No. I make it". The fear issue isn't really there. Probably it is more of a concern for actors. Anger, yes. Though I look at it (Building 8)

occasionally and hope nothing falls off. But that's a different kind of fear — very real — it's fear driven by the ubiquitous world of "Indemnity Insurance". Always with us.

Does there need to be a correspondence between the size of the idea and the size of the stage space, size of the building project?

No, I don't think so. The opportunity offered by scale, I suppose, is that in a slightly self-inflating way, you get to push a few ideas under a whole lot more noses. I do listen with interest, for example, to people who mention the building in conversation without provocation, and have opinions about, it to my face; maybe there's a social obligation of sorts there. There's something on the street line in Swanston Street that begins to impact on society — people who don't have opinions about public buildings, people who don't or haven't previously felt that architecture is capable of intervening in their lives, suddenly tell me Building 8 is making demands upon them — or maybe they're just poor conversationalists. Anyway, for good or for ill, it's there in Melbourne, and there's nothing quite like it in the rest of the country. Is it cause for rejoicing or concern? Well, the larger audience does hearten me. That's the best way to put it without sounding self-serving and thus decidedly unAustralian. In terms of size/scale, well opera's difficult because of the sums of money involved, thus it precludes most of your friends buying a ticket. Off-off Lygon Street is difficult — nobody can find the venues, not even in the newspapers, and the runs are short. So you work in a frustrating type of cultural ether: no matter how good the work is, it doesn't quite hit the mark — and never enough friends see it.

At the other end of the spectrum, and with similar difficulties, we find architecture ... I've always believed that architecture is at the heart of the debate, the social aesthetic debate, the social politic debate. If it were art for art's sake one would just go out to the back yard and weep.

Do you see linkages between any specific stage productions and Building 8? In raking over theatre projects which were happening contemporaneously with the genesis of Building 8, it struck me that there are quite distinct correlations that could be drawn between your design solutions for Belshazzar and the orientalism of your facade treatment. How do you respond to this kind of observation?

Yes, I think that's worth pursuing. As I think about it, they were both contemporaneous. Building 8's facade and a lot of the pre-thinking involved actually occurred subsequent to *Belshazzar*. I spent quite some time looking closely at Hedjuk's drawings as a source for the Handel. On the other hand, I think there was a war on in the Middle East (was there?), and Babylon was not the stuff of light discussion — certainly not building it on Swanston Street; though I was doing a little anarchistic posturing at the time, I suppose.

In terms of the investigation of forms in the cityscape constructed for Babylon and the facade solution for Building 8 and some of the elements making it up, there is a certain contiguity or a certain set of resonances in the forms that are employed in both. For instance, the tower and windmill-type elements that appeared in Belshazzar and the similar elements that float over the top of the building ...

Yes.

... it seems that there's a possibility that some of the sniffing around that would take place in designing a built vision of Babylon might also contribute to the ornamentalism and quite Byzantine approach to colour and pattern which appears on and throughout the building.

I'm not sure whether that's a question or whether it's an extremely astute statement. I'd bow to the latter.

For Belshazzar, were you looking at Oriental or Middle-Eastern archetypes?

Neither. The set was intended to be a hard, proud, representation of evil. *Belshazzar* was the image of failed evil; not the failure of faith. Just downright paganism. Not site specific.

So could Building 8 be a redemptive form of that?

Let's hope so. Yes, it's not inconceivable that, having watched *Belshazzar's* pagan immolation that I went back to the pallete and severely chastised myself. Redemptive is a charming complement. I would accept a correlation between those two projects, but it's the type of insight I would always expect from you, Michael, keenly astute and slightly disturbing.

What about the initial involvement in Gilgul, and the conscious focus that that required on transcendental issues, issues that are normally located in the realms of the theological dispute? Taking that on as a realm of investigation for theatre design had, in some repects, its antecedents in earlier architectural work in Keysborough and Box Hill, explorations of the theological issues or existential issues in built form.

Years ago, Harold Pinter's *The Birthday Party* impressed me as raising issues about the nature of what might be out there, awaiting us. Certainly, in that innocent era, existential questions had a great deal of currency — whether the individual could somehow be responsible for his own destiny. That has now been well and truly hosed down.

Working with the Gilgul group hardened my old resolve that theatre business and architecture business were not frivolous — Mies had said, "Architecture is not a cocktail". Big questions are faced. We don't necessarily resolve them, but we face them and we grow as human beings. Not necessarily better, but hopefully not worse.

There was a point when I decided in Building 8 that I would design every single staircase — the little juicy projects, usually passed off to ambitious juniors in big offices, spoils for the eager young designers — I took every single staircase and worked it very very hard. Now I think they're over-designed and quite clumsy on occasion, but there is a certain evangelical quality, an intensity. There was an attempt to try to make the staircases be answers, not questions.

What that might be involved once again is a consciousness of an audience. And perhaps if there's a parallel to be made between your recent theatre work and Building 8, it is that both require a certain kind of willing suspension of disbelief on the part of the viewer, where identification and enjoyment may be present, but these responses are somewhat distanced throught the degree of exaggeration, or the heightening, or the acceleration of visual devices that are employed.

I think that's a possible link with theatrical practice. Design and the idea of spectator acceptance, the distinction between appearance and reality. It's not a particular perceptual interest of mine. "Life size" on stage always fails — it's too small, every ASM knows that. Personally, I'd prefer to believe that the little bit extra should enable recognition, writ large, as it were; engage the audience, not hold them at arms' length. But "exaggeration" is not a word I would choose to use. Let's use "heighten".

The work in both arenas seems to hold out a visible challenge, and presents audiences with a "See what you can make of this!" attitude. That involves a certain distancing, I guess. It's overt rather than subtle.

Yes. I think it's important that the author/designer — in a theatrical sense — has a couple of "distancing" tricks/devices up his sleeve, that there is something behind the pantry door. We might wait for two acts until somebody opens the door and we discover that something has instead been in the closet, waiting. But these are old proven theatrical tricks, that are great fun, and work. They're essential to move a narrative. This necessary distance is understood in the theatre. But the culture of architecture nowadays is a culture of the surface, the skin, and increasingly so. You can see it vividly in furniture design, in the easy banalities of Starck. Boy, is that the design for our time!

With regard to the culture of the obvious, a way into comprehending the approach expressed by your theatre work and the approach expressed by Building 8 could be through characterising the work as camp. And I don't mean in terms of the gay sensibility, but more in terms of Sontag's shaping of notions of camp, whereby camp is an assertion of self-integrity, and an expression of a sort of temporary accommodation within society, whereby kitsch art becomes an intense mode of individualism, a form of spirited protest. In other words, it's beyond kitsch, beyond a mere celebration of casual excess, but a deliberate deployment of crude or offensive content to investigate ideas. How comfortable are you with the thought that your work could be characterised as camp?

No problem. I think the work is outside what's generally described as the present architectural aesthetic. Mark Twain once observed that Wagner's music was "better than it sounds". That was supposed to be a joke, but I think it's an interesting idea. I don't wish to sound petulant, but it's early in the morning. Aside from the aesthetic, all of the work is a personal obsession, outside of some debate going on elsewhere.

Sontag typifies camp in terms of its essential love of the unnatural, of artifice and exaggeration, and its expression of ironic and parodic appreciation of extravagant form that is out of proportion to content. Building 8 could have quite easily extruded the existing Glasshouse forms upwards, but your solution to this opportunity pushed well beyond its logical extremes, and the sort of playfulness and the sort of unwarranted excess that takes its form in the building could be characterised, if one were to try to categorise it, as a set of theatrical and high-camp gestures.

The final building envelope was actually quite strictly arrived at, it is simply the maximum development allowable. But the extravagant forms, well there's a piece of William Blake — and I was always very fond of Blake — one of his Proverbs of Hell, I think: *"A canary singing in a cage puts all Heaven in a rage".* That may be a clue.

I don't see Building 8 as having released the canary so much as having allowed it to sing.

Yes.

It has been suggested to me that it's possible to identify all kinds of finite conclusive examples of theatre form in the building: deliberate use of flattage, curtaining, screens and normative theatrical devices, but that doesn't interest me much.

Good.

Well, it's not as if you employ a set of standardised theatrical solutions in your stage work. I don't think I've seen a single flat. So there's a sort of redundancy that emerges when you try to transpose normalised concepts of what constitutes theatrical practice, theatrical devices. onto your built form, for when confronted by a theatrical problem or proposition, you don't turn to that repertoire of solutions.

When punters think about the theatre they tend to associate it with a music-hall image. In the mind, a curtain goes up and then a series of masking flats recede upstage to a great big cloth with a perspective painted on it. The scene diminishes over a series of hills to a lake beyond, and a fetching sky. That theatre exists in the minds of people who don't much go to the theatre. Personally, I can't really see much of it in the building. Theatre lighting, yes, I think; side-lighting through coloured glass, all that sort of thing. Where does the sun come up? Where's the light source? That sort of thing.

What about your use of colour with the steel curtain-wall out the back, where you set up what seems a deliberate pun through establishing a sort of trompe l'oeil curtain, a theatrical illusion.

There are probably some instances of the old-time theatrical colour schemes once produced by those lovely old scenic artists, who banged away on giant paint-frames at the back of Her Maj, or The Prinny. I did some scenic painting as a student. I'd like to think some of that colour shone through.

There is a recent job, however, that does have a very large coloured window. If you go outside at night with the lights on in the building, it's all there. It is genuinely scenic. John Gollings recently took some snaps. There was some water ponding in the plaza (which concerned me) and the window was reflected in it. The image was nearly Venetian; that lovely stained world-weary quality you found on Venetian facades. The Venetian light that results from the lagoon, the mist and the pollution in the air. This project does have a hint of scenic art about it. It's a shade romantic.

Well, mention of photography brings me to another possible correlation between your theatre work and your built work. It could be seen in your pursuit of the hyper-real. I'm interested in what kind of brief you give your photographers, because there's a consistent exploration of the theatrical in the way that your buildings are documented photographically.

Well there are two briefs. One that says "You're going to photograph a wedding — photograph everyone's face, photograph everyone smiling, photograph everyone with a drink in their hand", just to get a "carpet" photographic record. That's very hard nowadays with Gollings because he's gone off into zen-like certainty. He used to be more your basic *papparazzi.* The other instruction is to find the surreal moment. Not the artful realist moment, or the modern realist moment, or even the technical realist moment. John started to take the shots at night with assistants holding lamps, spots and floods, then he used coloured gels, and montage. He became possessed by the whole rigamarole; he pursued the dream, and to my horror started photographing everybody's work this way. He made all manner of buildings look metaphysical. This depressed me for quite some time. However, it was his right, and he was having great fun. I think of all those perspectives that Geoffrey (Barton) has done in the office, trying to isolate the building as an object, and examine it in the round as an object, not clutter it up with trees and cars and the usual graphic fodder. There may be a parallel somewhere between the drawings and John and his lens.

The imagery that you select to stake out an official public position for your built work seems to be imagery which lays out a quite self-consciously theatrical life for the buildings.

Well, yes I hope the buildings have "particular" and "special" lives. I suppose the images are not what you'd expect to discover as you turned from Barkly Street into Balaclava Road — familiar, but then not quite right. They are out of focus. I'd be happy if the buildings could inhabit dreams.

Well, therein lies the schism between the world of theatre and architecture, the disjunction. Do your buildings fail you because they are unable to create this world of dreams other than in photographic fantasy lives?

Fail, no. Disappoint, occasionally. (Divine to forgive, human to err and so on.) Fantasy lives are very important — they can be a source of sanity, a crutch. One has to consider what can be done within architecture, with budgets, with clients whose dreams as often as not outreach their financial capacities. Lately, I have occasionally been at a loss regarding expectations falling short. Maybe I'm just wearing out; or the ideal isn't the dream; or it's stamina, perhaps it is running a little thin. The construction manager on Building 8 referred to architects generically as bananas, with no great respect. I know what he means.

Leon van Schaik

Building 8:
The Appointment Process

Building 8 means a lot to RMIT. Its construction was an affirmation that RMIT was determined to be a university in the heart of the city; its successful completion signalled the way in which RMIT intended to address its facilities' needs; and it was the first physical manifestation of RMIT's mission as an international university.

The challenge was to create an appointment process that matched RMIT's mission statement, which made much of being at the forefront of technological innovation, and of excellence in graduate outcomes. Making a deft administrative move, David Wilmoth (chair of the committee) suggested that we flesh out this proposition with reference to

Those who want to set this story into a rigorous historical framework would do well to consult the history of RMIT that was published in celebration of its centenary:[1] mine is not an impartial view, I was there and have to tell this in terms of my experience.

The story of the reform of the consultant appointment process at RMIT began with a challenge to the University Campus Planning Committee[2] following what I believed to be the poor outcomes of the existing process.

the institution's strategic plan, and with the support of a ginger group of like thinkers.

My own views about the roles of consultants and their appointment were forged by several years as Chief Architect to the Urban Foundation (Transvaal Region). The Foundation focussed on community based projects, including self-help housing system design, and the provision of a full range of community facilities, from creches to parks. We tried a full range of consultant relationships, from in-house design, to direct appointment and to

[1] *Stephen Murray Smith and Anthony John Dare, The Tech: A Centenary History of the Royal Melbourne Institute of Technology, Hyland House Publishing, Melbourne, 1987.*

[2] *Then known as the Planning Committee, chaired by the Dean of Environmental Design and Construction.*

arms' length appointment by community groups using an agreed selection process. We also researched the experiences of other Foundations. This research, in conjunction with my own on-the-job learning about working with communities, brought me to the view that the best outcomes resulted from interactions between

identity strategy for RMIT, promoting in physical terms a future that matched the other arguments we had for being in the central business district of the city: location at the centre of the transport network; ready access for and to business and the professions whose members provided so much of the vocational punch of our courses.

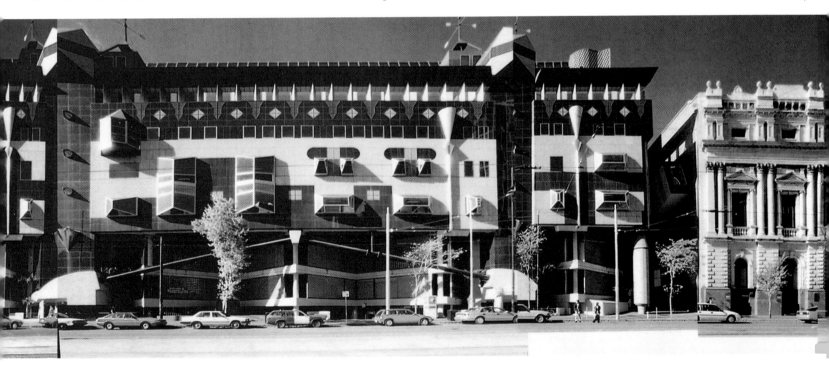

consultants and users where the appointment was made through an agreed selection process.

What emerged from our discussion at RMIT was a criterion based selection system — now generally termed "Quality Based Selection (QBS)". In a parallel overview of recent policy documents I discovered that the RMIT Centenary Commission had engaged a large number of prominent Melbourne thinkers in considering how the institution should relate to the city. This document readily became an articulation of a corporate

The strategy endorsed tangible relationships to the city and the "civic spine" of Swanston Street, and recommended that RMIT make overt its cultural contribution to the community.

Ruth Dunkin became the prime mover in the refinement and adoption of this QBS process and the corporate strategy. She had the strong support of David Beanland, an entrepreneurially oriented Director of RMIT. They provided the means (through a funded Capital Works strategy) to address RMIT's 40 per cent space shortfall on the

[3] Later a group (Dimity Reed, Sand Helsel and Chris Ryan, chaired by myself) charged with advising on a standing shortlist of architects, some for works below $2 million and requiring less proof of previous performance, but equal proof on other criteria, have proposed additional criteria (contribution to the educational process; ability to contribute to the corporate identity of RMIT, equal opportunity) in order to reduce the list of eligible practices to a manageable size.

[4] The centre city location was and is vital to the ability to attract a vigorous involvement by practitioners, always a strong point of RMIT's programmes.

City Campus. The selection process and criteria (demonstration of design excellence through awards, publications, exhibition; ability to relate to a complex user body; proven ability to design and deliver on time and within budget and such additional specific criteria as any particular project warranted) and the ideals behind it were adopted by the Capital Works Committee of Council, chaired by Don Little, and with the strong support of Dimity Reed, then a member of Council.[3]

A corrosive political fight for the survival of RMIT as a central city university serving the whole of Victoria and points beyond, was the

falling on deaf ears. A government planning document later shown to me, had the whole of our city campus zoned "Commercial".

As RMIT rejected the merger, the newly vitalised corporate strategy formed the conceptual basis for the brief for Building 8; the QBS system was activated; and in due course Edmond and Corrigan in association with the Demaine Partnership were appointed as the architects.

We had created a situation in which there was no double guessing, no expert committee of academics and functionaries "knowing better". We began to meet our educational ideals through our

[5] At a late stage a major user (Business) was relocated to another building. There was a six-week period in which to rejig the plans to include the faculty of Environmental Design and Construction in its entirety. As Alex Selenitsch shows, the brilliant planning of the large plates of the building anticipated such change, and accommodated it. Indeed, change will be continuous through the life of the building.

[6] Such as a vertical circulation system that does not always work well.

context for this work. Convinced of the importance of RMIT's leadership to the architectural culture of Melbourne,[4] I supported those at RMIT who opposed the manoeuvres that threatened our future presence in the city. While a proposed merger of RMIT and two small western institutions into a university of technology proceeded, David Beanland struggled in vain to persuade the interim council of this projected institution to purchase the downtown site of the Queen Victoria Hospital. It was mystifying but indicative to find our arguments

relationship with our consultants. User client committees worked with Maggie Edmond to establish the functional brief. The resolution of that brief into architecture was completely delegated to the architects. The commitment was widespread. In one politically dark moment, Ruth Dunkin said to me: "Whatever else happens, we will have left RMIT some very good buildings".

So it was that: "...the imaginative size of the building might be in some sort of relationship to the dreams of the client — the dreams and imaginative capacity of the client. It was a very unusual point in time at RMIT, there was a client able to articulate an ambition for the building" (Corrigan to Anderson).

The design process for Building 8 was subject to major changes,[5] and much that now seems perverse (such as the location and extent of the escalator bank) is the result of that history of change, and of how that change was managed. Another quotation, astonishingly spoken as another, perhaps even more interesting, institutional building (Ringwood Library) was nearing completion reflects this situation: "Maybe I'm just wearing out; or the ideal isn't the dream, or its stamina, perhaps it's running a

the general environment of change are unprintable. The statement that Corrigan quotes has to be seen for the self-justification that it so obviously is. It's not surprising that those who bear the brunt of operational problems[6] feel that the architects are a little less than omniscient. The fact that this Construction Manager went out of his way to over-ride user objections to this same system during the design stage, could not have eased his state of mind.

The dream survives the architects being called bananas: it is the Construction Manager who is now in exile in a Banana State, not the architect. Client and architect *were* well matched. RMIT

Photograph: John Gollings, May 1996.

little thin. The Construction Manager for Building 8 referred to architects generically as bananas, with no great respect" (Corrigan to Anderson). We can perhaps read in the context of the momentary despair of one partner the essential role of Maggie Edmond the other. Peter Slattery who controlled the very limited budget states that without Maggie, Building 8 could not have been completed.

While the Construction Manager might have been less than enthusiastic about architects, his views on

exists, it can be seen to exist. Its mission is made manifest, it has begun to play its proper role in its city. One building undid the neglect of a decade. It has been published world wide and RMIT has an image that matches the extent of its international reputation and the extent of its own ambitions. Opening it Paul Keating, Prime Minister, noted its congruity with the City Baths building, and claimed that Building 8 signalled Melbourne's return to a particularity of design excellence.

As RMIT continues to thrive, watch its space!

RMIT
CPC
SELECTION OF ARCHITECT FOR EXT TO BLDG E
RECOMMENDATION

GOAL : ~~TO~~ SIGNAL THAT RMIT is now committed
to design excellence and the optimum management
of its capital projects

OBJECTIVE : to appoint an architect
~~lead on the consultant team~~
with an internationally recognised
reputation for design excellence
based on Melbourne's design culture
and with the ability to maximise the
space & functional opportunities of Bldg E.

STRATEGY: to adopt a selection procedure
that calls for comparative analysis
of a selected short list of such architects,
and recommend for appointment
the architect most likely to achieve
the goal.

RECOMMENDATION : the committee recommends
that the firm of Edmond & Corrigan
working in association with the
Demaine Partnership be appointed
as the architects to Bldg E, and
that they now proceed to determine
the brief with the user client & the CPC.

REPORT : method : call for submission
· interview   ranking
· seeking of references
· seeking of legal info
· interview 2. re-ranking
Summary of findings

Draft recommendation to RMIT Council following selection process, penned on the back of a photocopy of a review of the "Korea" biography.